HORSEBACK GOSPEL

POEMS AND PRAYERS

Brad McClain

www.WildHorsePress.com

Dedication

First and foremost I dedicate the poems and prayers of this book to the Lord Jesus Christ who inspired them by His Spirit. To God be the glory!

Second, I dedicate this book to all those who have "liked," prayed for, and shared the Horseback Gospel Facebook Page with their friends. You have become a spiritual community that God is clearly using to change lives.

Finally, I dedicate this book to the men and women who live their lives the cowboy way. Some are horseback everyday and the rest would like to be! You know who you are.

God bless you and yours,

-Brad McClain

Special Thanks

We wish to thank award-winning cowboy artist, **Bruce Greene**, for giving his permission to use his beautiful painting for the front cover of this book. To see more of his work, go to: www.brucegreeneart.com. Thanks so much, partner!

Preface

While watching a commercial on the investment of gold, I noticed the actor was giving financial advice from the back of a beautiful horse. The idea came to me that sharing the good news of Jesus Christ while horseback might be effective in reaching people. I grew up in the cattle business and have ridden horses all my life, but always wondered if the Lord would use that part of my life to share Christ with others. A year of prayer preceded the launch of "Horseback Gospel," a website and Facebook page that, since June 10, 2014, has reached over 600,000 people from forty-five countries, with over 27,000 likes, and the numbers are still growing! (www.facebook.com/horsebackgospel) We post video devotionals, western art, scripture, music, poetry and prayers to plant spiritual seeds in the lives of people. The poetry and prayers have been especially well-received, so we decided to put some of them together in this book. We hope and pray the Lord will use them to bless your life. We encourage you to go online and "LIKE" Horseback Gospel, pray the Lord will continue to use it, and share it with your friends!

Yours for Horseback Gospel,
Brad McClain

Forward

I have never enjoyed the feelings of a Christian cowboy and pastor more than I have reading and sharing Brad McClain's poetry and scripture. You truly reach the western culture and integrity of all cowboy families. But most of all, you share the truth of our Lord.

Thank you, my friend and brother,
Tater Paschal
Pastor, Bosque County Cowboy Church
Clifton, Texas

First Published 2015

Copyright © 2015
By Brad McClain
Published By Wild Horse Press
An Imprint of Wild Horse Media Group
P.O. Box 331779
Fort Worth, Texas 76163
1-817-344-7036
www.WildHorseMedia.com
ALL RIGHTS RESERVED
1 2 3 4 5 6 7 8 9
ISBN-10: 1-940130-93-X
ISBN-13: 978-1-940130-93-4

Table of Contents

* Prayers

Real Cowboy

A cowboy is more
Than ridin' a horse,
Or tendin' the cattle,
That's part, of course.

But a cowboy is more,
Than boots and a hat,
Jeans, ropes, and buckles,
Much more than that.

And a cowboy is more,
Than the bars and the songs,
Dancin' and drinkin,'
A thousand gone-wrongs.

Real cowboys know
That what really matters,
Is chasin' a dream
When hopes are in tatters.

It's doin' a job,
From can until can't,
Discoverin' freedom,
When easy it ain't.

Livin' with rhythms,
Land and weather dictate,
The call of the rangeland,
An uncertain fate.

Doin' his best,
To be a good pard,
When storms are a-brewin,'
And the goin' is hard.

He gives his life,
To Jesus the Lord,
And trusts Him as Savior,
And believes the good Word.

And in the end,
When the loops are all throwed,
The whole herd is gathered,
And the broncs are all rode.

He hangs up his spurs,
And lays down his rope,
Unsaddles his pony,
And trusts in the hope,

That the Lord understands,
The real cowboy heart,
And opens the gate,
On a heavenly start.

"For by grace you have been saved
through faith, and that not of yourselves;
it is the gift of God." (Ephesians 2:8)

Listen

Cowboy: What do you want us to do, Lord?
God: Listen to your heart.
Cowboy: Sometimes I can't hear what my heart is saying.
What's the best way to listen?
God: Turn down the volume on the other stuff.
Cowboy: How?
God: Go saddle your horse...

Lariat of Love

God made His gather, but I was too wild,
To go with the round-up, and become His child.

I bolted and ran, thought I'd get away,
From the Savior who loved me, and called me to stay.

I jumped over fences, and broke through the gate,
At a fast pace to nowhere, refusing to wait.

Just bucking and kicking, and free to be me,
But the devil was waiting, no way I could see.

The pain he would give me, the guilt and regret,
The shame and the bondage, the traps that he set.

But the Lord has a long rope, and He rides a fast horse.
Thank God, never lost me, though I was off course.

Bone-tired and weary from the run that I made,
His grace finally reached me, on my trail He stayed.

He stood up in His stirrups, and sailed His loop true,
Then dallied down quickly, and turned me off, too.

The lariat of love brought me back from the brink,
Of all that destroyed me, nearly too late I think.

From the range of the hopeless and the devil's stampede,
To the field of forgiveness, and grace for my need.

Yes, He caught me and held me, and healed my deep hurt,
Then led me back with Him, and showed me my worth.

I now run with Jesus, and He's in control.
His brand's on my heart now, He lives in my soul.

The joy of God's pastures, with water that's clear,
And belly-deep forage, and freedom from fear.

But best of all blessings, is being at home,
With the One who pursues us, when we foolishly roam.

Praise God for salvation and being set free,
By Jesus who died and was raised just for me!
"But now in Christ Jesus you who were once far off have been brought
near by the blood of Christ." (Ephesians 2:13)

When the Devil Comes Callin'

When the devil comes callin', you'd best know what to do,
'Cause he's got some trouble that he wants to give you.

You might think it's easy, with his horns, tail, and smoke,
To know when he's comin', but this is no joke.

When he really wants you, he'll ride a nice horse,
His saddle's real shiny, and he's handsome of course.

His spurs are a'jingling, he's pressed nice and neat.
His voice is so soothing, you'll swear that he's sweet.

Or maybe a woman, all flirty and fun,
She's sexy and sassy, so you better just run.

He comes on all happy, shows you the best,
But he never is truthful, and hides all the rest.

The pain and the heartbreak, the guilt and regret,
The time that is wasted, what can't be reset.

And after he's stolen the best of your years,
You're busted and broken, and cried all your tears.

He'll cast you aside, on that that you can bet,
Rode hard to disaster, and turn you out wet.

God's Word clearly tells us, that when he appears,
He'll look like an angel, let those with ears, hear.

He tries to fool us, with his lying ways.
And that's why God's people should wise up and pray.

Put on God's armor, wear each piece in place.
Be strong in the Lord, and trust in His grace.

When he tries to throw up, what you did in the past,
Remind him of his future, and that God's Word will last.

Best of all just remember, when he comes to your door,
Let Jesus deal with him, and he'll hit the floor.

'Cause greater is He that lives within you,
Than any old devil. So rise up, it's true!
"Therefore submit to God. Resist the devil and he will flee from you."
(James 4:7)

✻⊞⅁

He Didn't Love Her

He didn't love her, he never could,
Though she believed it, she never should.

He was a cowboy, she took the bait,
He took advantage, she didn't wait.

Why did she do it? She did not know,
He never promised, to stay and not go.

She begged and badgered, he rode away,
Her heart was broken, she heard him say,

"Im gone to Calgary, and then to Cheyenne,
Don't know when I'll see you, I don't have a plan."

Nine months later, when the baby was born,
She hadn't seen him, by then she was torn,

By the joy and the challenge, of what she had done,
And the man she still prayed for, though he was long gone.

But then in a moment, everything changed,
'Cause the Lord has a plan, it's all pre-arranged.

It was on a cold Sunday, that the Lord touched his heart,
And the cowboy who left her, found a new start.

He took Jesus as Savior, and promised to give,
All his life for what matters, and always to live,

For the One who had saved him, and forgiven his sins,
To forgive those who hurt him, and go make amends.

He saddled the buckskin, determined to go,
And see the young woman, he didn't go slow.

She looked out of her window, he loped into view,
Stepped off of his pony, and somehow she knew.

He begged her forgiveness, and promised his love,
Told her the story, of his change from above.

He picked up the baby, that he'd never seen,
Said "I'll be the Daddy, that I've never been."

They were baptized together, by the preacher who came,
And all those who saw it, thought there is no shame,

When folks are forgiven, and they do the right thing,
The grace is amazing, of that we should sing.

The day of the wedding, was sunny and clear,
Like the vows that were spoken, so sweet and so dear.

This story happened, a long time ago,
But we should remember, 'cause we all need to know,

That the Lord has a plan, for all of His kids,
Even when we forget Him, and life's on the skids.

The grace for salvation, and to live a new life,
To parent our children, and be husband and wife.

"There is therefore now no condemnation to those who are in Christ
Jesus, who do not walk according to the flesh, but according to the Spirit."
(Romans 8:1)

Peace

Cowboy: Lord, will you give me peace and relief from stress?
God: Yes, but you have to let go of what is in your hands.
Cowboy: What do I have in my hands?
God: The reins...

God's Round Pen

When the worst really happens, and often it's true,
We can't seem to stop it, there's nothing to do.

Sickness and sadness, and troublesome times,
Deep valleys and darkness, and steep hills to climb.

There are those who can't stand it, they just run away,
Keep their sorrows inside them, make you think they're okay.

But they are just trying, to outrun the pain,
By avoiding the issue, think they can stay sane.

Like that old rank pony, nobody can ride,
'Cause someone abused him, and busted his hide.

The pain scarred his memory, and now he can't know,
That you're trying to help him, he's ornery and so,

He runs from the hand, that's gentle and kind,
Thinks you're going to hurt him, he's made up his mind.

But there's hope for most horses, no matter how wild,
If the trainer remembers, it's just like a child,

Who needs to be shown, the way he should go,
Not to hurt him or scare him, but to help him to grow.

There's hope for the wounded, and all that we feel,
Jesus died to forgive us, and our lives to heal.

It's just like the horseman, who knows what to do,
When the pony's too frightened to have any clue,

That this man is different, he's taking his time,
One step, then another, it'll work out just fine.

When we trust in the Savior, and respond to His grace,
He can heal all that hinders, and keep us in place.

He shows us the value, of what we've been through,
And works all to His glory, and for our good, too.

So if you're having, a really hard go,
Can't see the way forward, and answers won't show.

Remember that horse, that no one could tame,
Because of his problems, and history and pain.

He's now working cattle, and making a horse,
'Cause somebody helped him, to get back on course.

Just take it to Jesus, who said if you're through,
He'd give you relief, and strengthen you, too.

His yoke is easy, and His burden's light.
Cast all cares on Jesus, He'll make it all right.

So get in God's round pen, He'll know what to do,
You can trust in His method, His love makes us new.

"As you endure this divine discipline, remember that God is treating you as
His own children..." (Hebrews 12:7, NLT)

Forgive

Cowboy: Who should I forgive, Lord?
God: Everyone who has hurt you.
Cowboy: That's going to be hard to do. How?
God: Remember that I forgave you, and healed you by My stripes.
Cowboy: So when You heal me I can forgive?
God: You'll be healed when you're willing to forgive.
I'll even forgive through you if you're willing...

The Sun Rose

The sun rose this morning, and in its bold rays,
God's mercy rose with it, to bless the new day.

The birds sang His praises, as they flew along,
Greeting the dawning, with beautiful song.

The dogs came up wagging, and jumping about,
Not penned up but happy, and glad to be out.

The horses loped in, from their pasture of rest,
Full of the morning, and neighing with zest.

And now in the saddle, as I start the day,
The cattle are waiting, as if to say,

There's joy in the small things, that we have to do,
And best we remember, that God's in them, too.

The fence that needs fixing, re-stretch the wire tight,
The bull that needs penning, watch him, he'll fight!

The calf that looks puny, give him a good shot,
And go on and bring him, into the sick lot.

A quick break for lunch, way down by the creek,
Where you caught that big one, only last week.

Then back on my pony, to make a big round,
Through that distant section, gotta cover some ground.

And now the day's waning, and it starts to cool,
With their classes now over, kids get home from school.

Unsaddle my pony, and put him away,
Stop and think over, what happened today.

Lots to take care of, and try to get right,
And underneath feelings, that stay out of sight.

So much to remember, and be thankful for,
Be glad for our blessings, not driven for more.

The wind when it's blowing, and water that's clear,
A child's simple laughter, the things we hold dear.

The meal's on the table, and everyone's there,
We hold hands and bow, for Dad's simple prayer.

When supper is finished, and twilight comes on,
Day lingers a minute, it's here, then it's gone.

The night takes her place, the stars start to shine,
The moon rises slowly, all silky and fine.

And then the day's over, and we've done our best,
To finish the labor, and laid down to rest.

We'll whisper our thanks, to the good Lord above,
Who graces each day, with His presence and love.

"So I decided that there is nothing better than to enjoy food and drink and to find satisfaction in work. Then I realized these pleasures are from the hand of God..." (Ecclesiastes 2:24)

Grace

Cowboy: Lord, I don't understand Your love.
How can You love everyone the same?
God: Why do you ask?
Cowboy: Because it's hard to love some people
because of the way they act.
God: I don't love people based on how they act.
Cowboy: What is the basis for Your love?
God: I base My love, not on what they do, but on who I am.
Above all else, I am love, and that's how I love you.
It's called grace.

Cowboy Up

When I was a youngster, thought I'd grow up and be,
Nothing more than a cowboy, just wild and free.

I wish I knew then, what I now know today,
That life has its detours, it's all I can say.

But if you have ever, touched that way of life,
Far from the city, with its noise and its strife.

You never get over, what it feels like to be,
At home in the saddle, you love it, you see.

It's hard work and simply, being close to the land,
To husband the livestock, and make a top hand.

Your day starts real early, with coffee that's black,
And the dark shadows gather, before you get back.

There are cattle to doctor, and horses to train,
You're dry when its droughty, and wet when it rains.

You don't make much money, without much of a break,
But to the brand you are loyal, and you'll work for its sake.

I know there are those, who say that it's true,
That the cowboy is finished, but they don't say just who,

Will take care of the livestock, make use of the land,
In time with the seasons, and still make a stand,

For the free cowboy spirit, and all that it means,
Live close to creation, and follow your dreams.

I don't make my living, by working this way,
But I'm enough of a cowboy, to stand up and say,

It'll never be over, as long as we need,
Cattle there in the pasture, and some mouth to feed.

So you can't see that cowboy, or what fills his day,
He's too far from the asphalt, yes, he's miles away.

Off in the badlands, still riding the range,
Making his living, in a way that is strange,

To those who can't see, a life at that pace,
More critters than people, in a faraway place.

But he's part of the reason, this country is free,
He pledges allegiance, and means it, you see.

He's loyal to family, he makes a good friend,
He's kind to his horses, and strong to the end.

There's one other thing, that needs to be said,
And another good reason, this ought to be read.

And that is the closeness, that a real cowboy feels,
When he's out off the grid, God's near and He's real.

The love of a Savior, the strength of the Lord,
The peace of the Spirit, the light of His Word.

No you don't have to go there, to know that it's true.
But there's just enough cowboy, in me and in you,

To go back and discover, what real cowboys say,
It's not a great mystery, at the end of the day.

The direction we're headed, is the path that we choose,
Surrender to Jesus, or hold on and lose.

There's wisdom in seeing, that God has a way,
Cowboy up and get going, and don't wait a day.

"...If you confess with your mouth the Lord Jesus and believe in your heart
that God raised Him from the dead, you will be saved..." (Romans 10:9)

Beside the Campfire

The campfire sputtered, and began to burn low,
The long sunlight faded, the dark shadows grow.

The big herd was tired, they laid down to rest,
The day's drive was ended, each hand did his best,

To keep them from roaming, and getting away,
It took all we had, to drive them that day.

The night watch got started, and each took a turn,
The rest wrapped in blankets, and watched the fire burn.

Old Cookie came 'round, with biscuits and honey,
Some cowboys gambled, with buttons for money.

I asked the cow boss, if he could tell me,
Why some men turn outlaw, and some don't, you see.

He thought for a minute, then shook his head,
And I'll never forget, the words that he said.

"Some men just blow, like dust in the wind,
And never do see, that if they choose sin,

It's like planting seeds, not knowing what kind,
Of harvest will come, at a much later time.

They make themselves think, nobody will know,
And no one is hurt, by the bad seeds they sow.

But they are mistaken, and God's Word is true,
Bad choices we make, make bad harvest, too."

He then turned and looked, at me with a smile,
A tear in his eye, like I was his child.

"When a man gives his life to serving the Lord,
He depends on His Spirit, and trusts in His Word.

He learns to make choices, put seeds in the dirt,
That give righteous harvest, and healing, not hurt."

The old cowman smiled, and blew on his coffee,
I knew he was finished, and wouldn't be sorry,

To have some quiet moments, 'fore going to sleep,
Without any more questions, 'bout outlaws so deep.

The wind blew the treetops, the moon came up slow,
I remember like yesterday, though I'm old, you know.

It's been many years, since we drove up that trail,
I've seen lots of blessings, and my share of hell.

But one thing is certain, I always knew,
The right from the wrong, and how to stay true,

To the things my old trail boss, showed me and said,
That night by the campfire, 'fore we went to bed.

Yes, he was a Christian, and lived it each day,
Made clear by his actions, Jesus is the true way.

I've tried by His grace, to always sow seeds,
That glorify Jesus, and meet human needs.

Life isn't perfect, but one thing I know,
We can make a difference, just let the truth show.

It can be so simple, be ready to say,
What the Lord has done for you, and point to the way.

'Cause the Lord really saved me, from that outlaw trail,
Beside the old campfire, God's Word did not fail.

"Those who live only to satisfy their own sinful nature will harvest decay
and death from that sinful nature. But those who live to please the Spirit
will harvest everlasting life from the Spirit." (Galations 6:8, NLT)

The Bull-Rider's Prayer

He knew he'd prepared, for the big rodeo,
He practiced and prayed up, he was ready to go.

"Lord, if it's Your will, I need a big win,
I surrender it to You, I confess all my sin."

The bull that he drew, had never been rode.
He tried him in Denver, and in San Antone.

They called him "Old Charger," 'cause when you hit the ground,
He was coming back for you, thank God for the clown,

Who saved many riders, this bull tried to gore,
But who got away safely, though bruised up and sore.

Old Charger stood quiet, as he tightened the rope,
And got seated on him, holding onto the hope,

This this ride would give him, enough with a win,
To get to the finals, and finally begin,

To earn some real money, in the big time compete,
For the gold buckle, that would really be sweet!

He nodded for Charger, the bull came unglued,
But the cowboy stayed with him, with every wild move.

He swapped ends and twisted, he bucked and he spun,
It seemed like forever, that eight-second run.

But nothing Old Charger could do on that night,
Could throw the young cowboy, who stayed screwed on tight.

He even got in, a spur lick or two,
And then the horn sounded, and everyone knew,

That this was the ride, he hoped he would make,
In spite of the pressure, with so much at stake.

The cowboy went scrambling, Old Charger came back,
A ton of disaster, horns gleaming and black.

The rodeo clown, threw himself in the way,
To distract his attention, but the bull did not sway.

He zoned in on the cowboy, crowd came to their feet,
Old Charger was coming, to make up for defeat.

But at the last second, the bull stumbled and fell,
The cowboy escaped, and no one could tell,

Just why it had happened, no one could say,
They never had seen, a bull fall that way.

The angel stood quietly, in back of the pens,
Watching out for his cowboy, shaking everyone's hands.

The judge called the score, a big ninety-two,
It was all that was needed, the young cowboy knew,

That he got the answer, for what he had prayed,
He rode and he won, and escaped harm that day.

The bull hit that angel, that no one could see,
And couldn't go further, like hitting a tree.

So if you discover, that you're in a buck-out,
Dealing with problems, and battling with doubt.

Call on the Savior, just trust in the Lord,
He can deliver, rely on His Word.

He may send an angel, you just never know,
It happened before, at the big rodeo.

"For He shall give His angels charge over you, to keep you in all your ways." (Ps. 9:11, NKJV)

Old Blue

His eyes were blue, his gait was slow,
What he was thinking, he did not show.

For all those rides, I took before,
His trot was rough, a little sore,

Was all I got, and then one day,
Slack-reined and happy, all the way.

This horse blew up, he came unglued,
For no good reason, 'cept he was rude.

I thought of Buck, and Chris Cox, too,
Clinton Anderson, and what they knew.

Old Blue was crazed, I do not know,
But way up high, we both did go.

He buried his head, and left the ground,
All four feet, without a sound.

I was in shock, I held on tight,
He bucked again, with all his might.

I thought, O Lord, he's got to stop,
But I was wrong, he bucked a lot.

Then I knew, I would be tossed,
When my stirrup, on the left I lost.

I thought, bale out, get off this fool,
But I forgot, that safety rule,

That if you find, you must let go,
Do not do it, until he's low.

But when I did, he sailed up high,
For a second, I touched the sky.

But then a storm, of gravity,
Took me down, and planted me.

On the hard ground, oh my it hurt,
I could not move, there in the dirt.

My brother laughed, but then he knew,
He could see, as my pain grew,

That this was worse, than when before,
I got bucked off, and rode some more.

I could not stand, he got the truck,
Took me to town, and dern the luck.

My pelvis broke, and my hip, too,
Busted ribs, this much I knew,

That it would take, some time to heal,
Weeks in bed, that was the deal.

I wondered why, I prayed a lot,
And the first word, that I got,

Was that I did not, really know,
My true need, to hear and grow.

I had a little, argument,
With this word, that Jesus sent.

I thought I listened, carefully,
And tried to do, what He said to me.

But then that verse, came to mind,
That Jesus quoted, 'bout the time,

Alone with Him, the devil said,
Do a trick, make these stones bread.

Man shall not live, with just our bread,
But by God's word, that's what He said.

It hit me hard, that just how true,
This counsel was, and what to do.

He will tell me, what I need,
To live God's way, and plant the seed,

For future harvest, and the way,
To do God's will, and everyday.

I had to wonder, that if I chose,
To listen better, the day I rose,

To ride Old Blue, that bucked that day,
And broke me up, would Jesus say,

"Don't bother going, at home just stay,
For you'll get hurt, if you ride today."

I'm not certain, don't really know,
But one thing's sure, before I go,

I now listen, in a brand new way,
So I can hear Him, if He wants to say,

Don't do this, or now go there,
The Spirit leads, He wants to share,

All that we need, to do God's will,
Apply God's Word, be Spirit-filled.

Old Blue they sold, I do not know,
Just where or who, a rodeo?

And I've been well, for quite some time,
But won't forget, that simple line.

The words God speaks, are what we need,
If we will listen, He will lead.

"...Man shall not live by bread alone; but man lives by every word that proceeds from the mouth of the Lord." (Deut. 8:3, NKJV)

Old Cowboy

I saw him when, he hit the door,
And made his way, across the floor,

Of the small cafe, where we planned to meet,
He saw my wave, I stood to my feet.

His shirt collar, was buttoned up,
Wore brand-new jeans, turned up a cuff.

The cowboy hat, upon his head,
Was sharply creased, his scarf was red.

He walked with a limp, but straight as could be,
His eyes were clear, when he looked at me.

His grip was strong, hands leather-tough,
He looked as if, he'd seen enough,

Of life out there, with weather and land,
To talk to me, this old cow-hand.

The steak he ate, in record time,
Sipped his coffee, said it was fine,

To ask about, the work he'd done,
Since coming here in '61.

We talked about, horses he rode,
Some topped off, sometimes throwed.

Of ropes and races, and real bad wrecks,
Hopes held high, and bouncing checks.

He spoke of cows, that got away,
Of loops that missed, and penning strays.

He talked about, a big red roan,
The very best, he ever owned.

And how this horse, had made a friend,
And gave his best, until the end.

His eyes got wet, when he told of when,
His wife got sick, passed on and then,

Their only son, went off to fight.
A road-side bomb, took his life.

He showed me shots, of both of them,
And times they laughed, and even then,

He seemed to want, to tell me more,
I hoped he'd say, what I came for.

You see I knew, about the past,
What people said, the rumors last.

How he was, a young outlaw,
Bad to fight, quick on the draw.

They say he'd killed, a dozen men,
Though none could say, just how or when.

I knew for one, he'd done some time,
A governor's pardon, cut short the fine.

And now he was, a hundred three,
I can't believe, he talked with me.

His voice got low, He asked if I,
Believed in God, I asked him why.

Because he said, unless we do,
Life can't make sense, it's really true.

He said that as, a younger man,
He never knew, God had a plan.

But through the years, he'd come to know,
The Lord is real, and wants to show,

His love to all, forgive our sin,
Give us peace, and let Him in.

He said, "Now, son, remember that,"
As he stood, picked up his hat.

He gripped my hand, I heard him say,
"Before I go, just let me pray."

With simple words, he prayed for me,
That Christ would come, and set me free.

Then out the door, and on his horse,
No car to drive, too old of course.

But I cannot, forget that day,
Or the words, I heard him say.

An old cowboy, who helped me see,
All that God had done for me.

"This is a faithful saying and worthy of all acceptance, that Christ Jesus
came into the world to save sinners, of whom I am chief."
(1 Tim. 2:15, NKJV)

Hypocrites

Cowboy: Lord, people say they don't go to church because of the hypocrites.

God: I understand. I have a problem with hypocrites, too.

Cowboy: So what should I say to them?

God: Tell them I said I'd rather them go to church with some of the hypocrites than go to hell with all of them...

Older

There's coming a day, I know it, it's true,
When I won't be able, to do what I do.

I hate to admit it, it's called getting old,
A cowboy can feel it, don't have to be told.

Your joints get all stiff, and the lines on your face,
Look like a road map, all over the place.

The times when you crashed, all start to hurt,
All that old damage, when you hit the dirt.

You search for a horse, that isn't so tall,
Dead broke and gentle, from which you won't fall.

You watch what you're doing, don't move quite so fast,
And savor the moments, make everything last.

Got nothing to prove, at home in your skin,
Don't have to control things, you know where you've been.

Sometimes you get wishful, for the wild days of youth,
When the horses were faster, but to tell you the truth,

You wouldn't go back, and start over again,
'Cause what you now know, has value and then,

The world just isn't, the same as before,
Right and wrong was more simple, they'd show you the door.

'Cause you never did learn, to be politically correct,
Just say what you mean, that's it- what the heck!

God knows that this temple, belongs just to Him,
He helps us to follow, and stay clear of sin.

I think when He sees me, He knows that I try,
To be filled with the Spirit, and will till I die.

And maybe, just maybe, when I'm eighty-eight,
I'll still lead my pony, on out through the gate.

Ask God for the strength, to mount up and ride,
Stay focused on Jesus, and with Him abide.

"Now may the Lord direct your hearts into the love of God and into the patience of Christ." (2 Thess. 3:5, NKJV)

Off the Grid

My horse stamps his feet, and all I can hear,
Are his quiet movements, as he stands there so near.

I'm off in the country, I came here to pray.
I've lifted my family, and promised to stay,

Faithful to lead them, and always be true,
Prayed for the wisdom, to know what to do.

When all you can hear, are the sounds of the night,
The Lord speaks His whisper, and says it's all right,

To lay down our burdens, and rest for awhile,
Know that He's with us, and enjoy His smile.

I pray for our nation, and our leaders, too.
For our military, who go, serve, and do,

What they are ordered, so we can live free,
With godly blessing, be the best we can be.

I pray for the people, my partners and friends,
Those who serve with me, who seek the same ends.

I pray for the lost ones, who haven't come home,
That they will find Jesus, and never more roam.

I pray for the nightmares, this world is full of,
And ask God for mercy, and fill us with love.

So we can do something, even if it is small,
We can make some difference, and not drop the ball.

The breeze cools the campsite, and sings in the trees,
The wind of the Spirit, with Him I agree.

The coals of the campfire, are burning down low,
My body grows weary, I'm ready to go,

Find rest till the morning, and then rise to see,
Not just the dawning, but mercy to be,

All He has planned, for the new day,
Saddled and ready, we'll do it His way!

Thank God for the time, spent alone with the Lord,
Praying and praising, and reading His Word.

With God there is nothing, that we cannot do,
If to the Spirit, and the Word we are true.

Now we are moving, down the trail we must go,
Trusting in Jesus, the way He will show.

Back to the battle, yes, back to the fight,
Be strong in the Lord, and rely on His might.

So if you are weary, tired and stressed out,
Please just remember, what it's all about.

Just run to Jesus, and lay down your care,
Get off the grid, and if not, anywhere!

"Draw near to God and He will draw near to you..." James 4:8

One Good Horse

I saw the ad, and made the call,
A horse for sale, fifteen hands tall.

A quarter horse, a registered gray,
Seasoned gelding, all the way.

Don't think that gal, knew what she had,
Just out of cash, and feeling bad,

That the horse was thin, and she was strapped,
To keep him fed, and that was that.

I liked his look, well-built and straight,
He nuzzled my hand, I could hardly wait,

So I saddled him up, and took a good ride,
I got excited, but tried to hide,

The way I felt about this horse,
And how he moved, and turned of course.

I stepped off and asked if he,
Could be used to rope, the cattle you see.

She did not know, so I made the request,
To test him out, she'd do her best,

To have him at the roping pen,
I told her where, what night and when.

On the very edge of Old Cowtown,
There's a place to rope, they come around.

Pay their cash, and run the steers,
Get practiced up, without the fears,

Of poorly roping, in front of a crowd,
Just take your shots, no one gets loud.

Score the cattle, make your run,
Get back in line, for your next one.

I backed Old Gray, beside the steer,
They let him go, he hit a gear.

Put me right there, I threw my line,
And turned him off, it worked just fine.

By the time, we roped some more,
I knew I'd found, what I looked for.

I wrote the check, with a great big smile,
Got him home, and spent awhile,

Thanking the Lord, for helping me find,
A horse that became, a friend of mine.

For many years, he was the one,
That took me to, the winning run.

But bigger still, was something true,
It seemed he knew, just what to do,

When all I had, was a broken heart,
No one to care, and take my part.

He'd look at me, and seem to say,
This too will pass, you'll be okay.

I know that some, won't understand,
The way I felt, no doubt they can,

Find better ways, to overcome,
The trials of life, and get things done.

Think what you will, but I believe,
Old Gray was sent, so I'd receive,

What I needed, that time in life,
Filled with sorrow, and lots of strife.

And isn't it, just like the Lord,
To teach that we, can trust His Word.

That says He will, give what we need,
For every problem, just let Him lead.

Jamaica Drifter, that was his name.
Sounds exotic, and he came,

At just that time, and now he's gone,
And I am left to get along,

Without that friend, who helped me out,
But God is good, there is no doubt.

They say in life, if you can find,
One good horse, he'll ease your mind.

But better still, that we can know,
God's grace is real, He lets it show.

"...My grace is sufficient for you, for My strength is made perfect in your
weakness..." (2 Cor. 12:9)

If God Made a Rope

If God made a rope, to catch me and you,
I think He'd be careful, with what He would use.

The strands would be sturdy, with hope woven in,
'Cause without it there's nothing, nowhere to begin.

Yessir, hope would be there, used as a start,
For getting a lariat, to capture our heart.

Though hope gets us started, it's not really sure,
Of the thing that is promised, but when it endures,

The truth transforms hope, to something that's certain,
It becomes faith, which opens the curtain.

Yes, the rope needs faith, because it's a key
For pleasing the Savior, for blind eyes to see,

All that God shows us, and wants us to know,
Faith wraps the hope strands, with assurance that grows.

But the rope isn't finished, with just these two things,
There's one something more, that gives it its wings.

And that is the strand, of God's holy love,
Manifested in Jesus, and sent from above.

Without love the rope, would be much too weak,
To catch all the strays, with a strong stubborn streak.

Yes, the strength that love adds, to the rope that God makes,
Is the thing that pursues us, whatever it takes.

And when the rope finally settles, and gets hold of our hearts,
Hope, faith and love touch us, even in the deep parts.

We're led to the Savior, who gives us new life,
Casts out all our fears, and calms down our strife.

We're glad to be captured, and finally see,
That when Jesus takes over, we're really set free!

"Three things will last forever- faith, hope,
and love- and the greatest of these is love."
(1 Cor. 13:13)

Cotton-Eyed Joe

Early that spring, the new colts were born,
One little bay stud, and looking forlorn.

Slight little sliver, of white round his eye,
Small white snip, on the nose made me sigh.

What shall we name him, don't really know.
Guess it'll be, Cotton-Eyed Joe.

When I first saw him, I thought he might be,
The kind of a cow horse, we all want to see.

Got gelded and branded, when he turned one,
Broke to the halter, then turned out to run,

Another full year, in the pastures so strong,
And then he turned two, it wouldn't be long,

Before we would pen him, and bring him along,
Pony him 'round, with a big cousin strong.

Got our hands on him, and gentled him right,
Sacked out and worked him, and dealt with his fright.

Taught him to trust us, trained him to lead,
Lots of good ground work, brought him up to speed.

Now go get the saddle, and see what he'll do,
Time to get on him, a real buckaroo.

But he stood real quiet, and never did buck,
We were so thankful, with that kind of luck.

Rode out of the round pen, just walking real slow,
That's when we learned, about Cotton-Eyed Joe.

He went from a walk, to a buck with no sound,
And after four jumps, I hit the ground.

We led him around, and I stepped back on,
He never minded, looked like we had won.

The more I rode Joe, the better he got.
We went and worked cattle, I liked him a lot.

He neck-reined and stopped, backed up and turned,
Load on the trailer, all this quickly learned.

I roped a sick yearling, Joe knew what to do,
But he started pitching, came untrained, too.

And every so often, while doing his work,
He just took a notion, to buck and to jerk.

One time we were checking, a pasture all day,
For no good reason, he put me away.

Went from a walk, with a slack rein,
To a high-flying bronc, and nothing to blame.

He threw me and stopped, did not run away,
Just looked at me there, as if to say,

I can still throw you, if I want to,
You cannot stop me, whatever you do.

The thing about Joe, try as we might,
To make him buck, he responded just right.

Could not make him do it, calm as could be,
Until he decided, to surprise us you see.

Penning some cattle, that tried to turn back,
Joe was a fast one, threw him some slack.

And just like a scene, from an old rodeo,
That horse took a notion, to put on a show.

He bucked and he pitched, and tried to swap ends,
My cinches were broken, they both came unhinged.

I rode Billy Cook, right down to the ground,
My hat hit an ant bed, my mouth made no sound,

Because it was filled, with mud and manure.
Joe was the winner, it was hard to endure.

We did more ground work, and many more miles,
Joe was a stout one, made everyone smile.

But just when we thought, he was through with his game,
He'd cut loose bucking, it was always the same.

A young cowboy came by, our ranch one fine day,
Looking to buy, a horse that would stay,

Right on the cattle, he dogged to the ground.
We thought of Joe, and led him around.

That gelding was pretty, well-built and straight,
The cowboy sure liked him, when we opened the gate.

He stepped on and rode him, we had high hope,
That Joe wouldn't throw him, as he started to lope.

Joe acted just perfect, as calm as could be,
Not one bad habit, that any could see.

We told him the truth, about Joe that day,
That sometimes he bucked, and we couldn't say,

Just why he did it, he just wanted to,
So if you buy him, expect it, it's true.

We got our money, Joe was easy to load,
Cowboy drove past the round pen, and on down the road.

And that's the last time, I ever did see,
Cotton-Eyed Joe, I wondered if he,

Bucked the guy off, when he got him home,
Or waited awhile, let him ride some.

When I think about it, this much comes to me,
I'm like that colt, just like him, you see.

Even though I, have long known the Lord,
Served in the Lord's work, taught others His Word.

I still can do some things, that surprise even me,
And disobey Jesus, with Him disagree.

I've had some good training, but in spite of it all,
Am prone to come untrained, into selfishness fall.

As with a good horse, that you count on to be,
The same every trip, it's consistency.

We need to be faithful, and ask the Lord how,
To consistently serve Him, we need to start now.

"I say then: Walk in the Spirit, and you shall not fulfill the lust of the flesh." (Gal. 5:16, NKJV)

Off to Cheyenne

Off to Cheyenne,
For the big rodeo.
Daddy of all of 'em,
Get ready, let's go!

With cowboy stuff packed,
And so much to see,
I can't help but wonder,
How will it be?

In the high-plains arena,
Rip-roaring fun,
Bulls and horses that buck,
Roping stock on the run.

The best of the west,
Compete for the cash,
While the rest of us holler,
And watch the mad dash.

We'll hoot and we'll laugh,
At the ones that buck off,
But be glad we're too old,
To ride the rough stuff.

We'll look at the horses,
Did you see the way,
That big buckskin moves,
Or maybe that gray?

Can't miss cowboy church,
R.W. will sing,
We'll hear the gospel,
Yes, it's the real thing.

We'll take it all in
And not waste a minute,
And dream of the time,
When we were still in it.

And in a real way,
We've always been,
'Cause when you're raised horseback,
It runs deep within.

When the party's all over,
And we pack up to go,
We'll remember the good time,
At the big rodeo.

We'll get back to the schedule,
And back to our tasks,
But a part of ourselves,
If anyone asks,

Will be left on the high plains,
In a place called Cheyenne,
Where we went that summer,
And cowboyed and ran.

"Every good and perfect gift is from
above, and comes down from the
Father of lights..." (James 1:17)

Pain

Cowboy: Why is this so painful, Lord?
God: Because you care.
Cowboy: Is it better if I don't care?
God: No, I want you to care.
Cowboy: What about the pain?
God: Cast all your care on Me, for I care for you...

Corky

When I was just five, my Dad said, "Come, see,"
He led out a horse, that was meant just for me.

I'd ridden a pony, at the young age of three,
Now I'd have a real horse, he was something to see.

A big, rangy gelding, black with a blaze,
His name was Corky, thought I'd ride him always.

I couldn't get on him, without help of course.
I used the fence, to get on my horse.

He always just stood there, and waited for me,
Never got rattled, so patient you see.

They say he was named, for a steer wrestling man,
With one leg of cork, who still made a hand.

He'd ridden Corky, to all the big shows,
And then he retired, no more rodeos.

His kids then rode Corky, and now he was mine,
A gentler old pony, my Dad could not find.

He seemed to know, kids new at this stuff,
Couldn't do him much damage, that old horse was tough.

He'd still watch the cattle, and turn when he should,
Though he was past twenty, he showed that he could.

I spent many hours, just learning from him.
He taught me to ride, work cattle and then,

Go through a childhood, that most kids don't know,
Way out in the country, where I grew up and so,

I remember the days, though so long ago,
When I saddled Corky, and away we would go.

I learned to ride pasture, and check on the fence,
Pen any sick cattle, and learn to make sense,

Of a business that's run, with weather and land,
Unpredictable factors, do the job of a hand.

Fix fences when needed, rope sick yearlings, too,
Doctor them up, and know what to do.

And so the years passed, and Corky turned gray,
He slowed down a lot, I remember the day,

That family came over, to look at my horse,
Kids both excited, our Dads talked of course.

"I need to have something, that my kids can ride,
He's got to be gentle, Dan's seven, Lynn's five."

My Dad looked at me, said "What do we do?
Can you let him go, so they can learn too?"

It was seven great years, that I'd spent with him,
If I am a cowboy, that horse broke me in.

I handed the lead rope, to the boy with smile,
And walked away quickly, to think for awhile.

They opened their trailer, he was easy to load,
Off to make memories, and on down the road.

I've thought many times, and even today,
When best gifts are given, then given away,

The lesson of Corky, is one we should learn,
Enjoy what we get, then when it's our turn,

Pass on to the next one, what we have received,
To lovingly share, shows what we believe.

We're blessed with so much, but this much is true,
If we try to hoard it, we just lose it, too.

Blessed by the good Lord, a blessing to be,
Freely receive it, then give just as free.

"...Freely you have received, freely give..." (Matt. 10:8, NKJV)

When I Think of Dad

When I think of Dad, I think of the work,
He did all his life, he never did shirk.

From the start of the day, he never slowed down,
Until he was finished, he made every round.

Fought in the war, came home and then,
Married my mother, a new life to begin.

He bought him a ranch, with his VA loan,
Cleared it himself, and built them a home.

Bought and sold cattle, stayed busy, and he,
Made every auction, a cowman to be.

Twenty-plus orders, that he had to fill,
Cattle shipped westward, that was the deal.

Expanded the business, leased lots of land,
Stocked it with yearlings, made a strong stand.

We got the bull yearlings, in the fall of the year,
Made steers of them, then kept them near,

Until they were ready, in the pastures turn out,
Then a year later, by then full and stout,

We gathered them up, and shipped them to feed,
Then brought in the new ones, like planting the seed,

Of a harvest we gathered, with care every time,
In good and bad weather, no matter what kind.

Some years made money, and others not so,
He had friendly bankers, who financed his go.

The horses I rode, he bought and we used,
From Oklahoma, and west Texas, too.

He wasn't a hugger, did not hear him say,
I love you too often, the work filled his day.

Sometimes he was angry, could not satisfy,
You might not could do it, but you better try.

So I grew up the son, of a cowman you see,
And thought that I, would evermore be,

The cowboy who rode, and stayed with the land,
Just tending the livestock, and making a hand.

Guess you could say, that I am surprised,
By all that happened, in our family's lives.

The land that Dad worked, so hard to see,
Is no longer ours, it's gone, so is he.

My mother's still with us, and doing quite well,
Though she's in her eighties, you really can't tell.

I guess all that matters, is what Dad left me,
A strong working ethic, it's helped me to be,

The man I became, and what I'll become,
For those who come after, my daughters and sons.

He was not perfect, about many things wrong,
But even his mistakes, have helped me be strong.

I believe he's in heaven, because of belief,
In the Lord Jesus, that gives me relief.

And many a time, the words that I say,
Sound just like he said it, almost everyday.

Yes, I am the son, of a strong cattleman,
And what I learned from him, helps me make my stand.

"Honor your father and mother, which is the first commandment with
promise: that it may be well with you and you may live long on the earth."
(Eph. 6:2-3)

Big Boy

Just a little old puppy, when Dad brought him home,
Just barely weaned, but already winsome.

I could not know, when I saw him there,
The adventures I'd have, and with this dog share.

An English shepherd, all black and white,
We named him Big Boy, it fit him just right.

We had dogs for hunting, to track cattle, too,
But Big Boy had one job, to protect me and you.

Yes, he was the watch dog, that kept us all safe,
And if we were threatened, he wouldn't wait.

He had a low growl, that sure meant a fight,
Most times he barked, but sometimes he'd bite.

But he was my pal, and we had great fun,
Running and playing, in the long summer sun.

I learned to ride horses, on Big Boy you see,
He was so big, he could carry me.

But then I got older, and gained a few pounds,
Big Boy nipped at me, I fell to the ground.

It just broke the skin, and Mom always used,
Good on merthiolate, bottled child abuse!

She then called Doc Nolan, who told her that she,
Should pen up the dog, to check for rabies.

She hung up the phone, asked "which dog bit you?"
And when she asked it, I could not tell the truth.

I had just watched a movie, made by Disney,
It's called "Old Yeller," 'bout a dog with rabies.

And I knew Old Yeller, had to be killed,
I had to save Big Boy, not let him be drilled.

So I told a big one, did not bat an eye,
"It was a beagle," my very first lie.

And that's when the trouble, really began,
The dog that I mentioned, from the house ran.

We could not find him, though we searched everywhere,
And all through the process, Big Boy was right there.

Next day the Doc, said all we could do,
Was bring in your son, to have shots, it's true.

So for two weeks, on each single day,
Got a shot in my stomach, to make me okay.

And I never told them, the truth right away,
I thought I'd best wait, for just the right day.

I'll never have rabies, that's good I guess,
But that lie that I told, made a big mess.

I was in college, when I finally came clean,
By then no one cared, or that's how it seemed.

But I'll tell you what, I learned from that chore,
The truth might get painful, but lies hurt much more.

"If you want to enjoy life and see many happy days, keep your tongue from speaking evil and your lips from telling lies." (1 Peter 3:10)

Prodigal

"I'm gone, I"m through, I'm out of here!"
My Dad was angry, Mom shed a tear.

I thought I knew something, that I didn't know,
'Bout how to be happy, it was all about go.

I was through with the ranch, and all my Dad's rules,
Gone from the hard work, and away from the fools,

Who spend their lives working, from can until can't,
And if you don't do it, hear my Dad rant.

Tired of the branding, and cutting bulls,
Fixing the windmills, keeping tanks full.

Fighting the weather, doctoring cows,
Pulling the calves, and save them somehow.

So off from the boondocks, and on into town,
Thinking I'd party, and make all the rounds.

I had some money, that I'd put away,
From selling cattle, and friends' roundup days.

I found out the cash, could buy lots of fun,
Women and drinks, and drugs while you run.

I stayed so messed up, most of the time,
I had no conscience, or reason, or rhyme.

I can remember, when I sold my bay,
Along with my saddle, just so I could stay,

And gamble one night, before I was through,
And then I was dead-broke, and wondered who,

Would give me a dollar, or someplace to go,
Cold in the desert, and the neon's harsh glow.

A man who got garbage, to feed to his swine,
Said "Come on and help me, you'll do just fine."

The restaurants in Vegas, gave it to him,
He'd pick up, then feed it, to the hogs in his pens.

I got so hungry, I picked through the feed,
To try to find something, for me fit to eat.

And then I remembered, all of those hands,
Who worked for my father, and followed his plans.

I thought I had better, get on back home,
And just ask my Daddy, if he had some,

Work for a fellow, who'd been such a fool,
Who left all the good things, and broke all the rules.

I made up a speech, inside of my mind,
What I'd say to him, if he had the time.

Took me awhile, to go all the way,
Just riding my thumb, and no place to stay.

But I finally got there, and opened the gate,
With the sun setting, I picked up my pace.

And then I saw someone, coming toward me,
At a full gallop, it was something to see.

Here came my Daddy, with tears in his eyes,
Jumped off his pony, and to my surprise,

Threw his arms round me, and would not let go,
Made me ride with him, we didn't go slow.

I tried to tell him, how sorry I was,
For leaving the ranch, and hurting the cause,

Of all that my family, had always stood for,
Love God and country, don't ask for more.

But Dad wouldn't listen, and all he could say,
Was "let's have a party!" We did it his way,

With music and dancing, and good bar-b-q,
And all that he even, wanted to do,

Was talk of the son, who had come home,
That was alive, not dead and undone.

Big brother came in, with his trailer and truck,
Unloaded his pony, and then asked "what's up,

With this music and party, and all of this fun?"
They said that I'd come home, and what Dad had done.

But he was so mad, that Dad was so kind,
He wouldn't join in, he made up his mind.

Guess you can live, at the father's, you see,
But not have his spirit, or with him agree.

We all need compassion, we've all done our sin,
But when we return, from where we have been,

We'll find there's a Daddy, whose heart will forgive,
And throw a party, for those who will live,

In the good pastures, and place He has planned,
Live with His blessing and obey His commands.

"...Kill the fatted calf we have been fattening. We must celebrate with a feast, for this son of mine was dead and has now returned to life. He was lost, but now he is found. So the party began..." (Luke 15:23-24)

My Dad's Hands

I remember so well, when I was a lad,
Times long ago, spent with my Dad.

A rancher, a cowman, a trader was he,
And that's all I ever, thought I would be.

He was one of those men, who had a strong grip,
And if you worked with him, you better not slip.

With a gun or a knife, or a tool you could see,
His hands had the skill, to know where to be.

Look a man in the eye, give a firm shake,
And don't look away, that's what he would say.

When he took my arm, and said what to do,
I had the sense, to stop 'cause I knew,

I didn't want him, to take hold of me,
If I was too stubborn, to listen and see.

I sat beside him, and looked at his hands,
While we were in church, the hands of a man.

I traced the lines, and callouses there,
Tanned by the sun, on the back lots of hair.

Sitting there with him, with his hand in mine,
I'd almost forgotten, the strength of that time.

I know that I wanted, my hands both to be,
Just like my Daddy's, for all to see.

Time passes quickly, my childhood went by.
I had my heart-breaks, got too tired to cry.

Running from all, I knew that was right,
Wasting my time in the dark, not the light.

But in the quiet, the Savior who came,
Showed me He loved me, and called out my name.

I looked at the hand, outstretched to me,
Traced the lines in it, surprised to see,

The callouses of, a hard-working man,
And there in the center, the scars in his hand.

And now that I've found Him, I will not let go.
Because He's the One, I needed to know.

And I want these hands, to be His you see,
Follow Him now, and eternally.

"Then He said to Thomas, 'Put your finger here, and look at my hands...'"
(John 20:27)

Jesus' Birthday

Cowboy: Did we do okay with Jesus' birthday, Lord?
God: Did you have a day of love and peace?
Cowboy: Yes, because we had Your love that never fails and
Your peace that passes all understanding.
Can we have another one?
God: Yes, you can have one everyday...

The Neighbor's Bull

My brother's friend, had him some cows,
That our neighbor's bull, so liked somehow,

That he would never, leave them alone,
Kept getting out, and wouldn't come home.

He weighed about, one thousand pounds,
A brangus bull, they had a round,

Of talk about, just what they should do,
My brother said, this much is true,

Aren't ya'll thinking, it makes some sense,
To take some time, to work on the fence?

They spent the cash, and fixed it right,
Pulled all the wire, and stretched it tight.

And now just one thing, we need to get done,
Go get the bull, that's been on the run.

I got the call, I said that I'd come,
And help him out, no problem, son.

Our plan was simple, go find the sport,
Ride into the pasture, and make the sort.

Then drive the bull, out through the front gate,
And down the road, no need to wait.

We found the bull, in a brushy place,
Threw up his head, and found a space,

With those old cows, he'd loved so long,
Thought he could hide, but he was wrong.

We cut him out, and on the run,
Back through the woods, gonna be fun.

And almost out, we thought we're through,
But he had one more, trick he would do.

Turned from the gate, he changed his mind,
Back to the cows, he left behind.

We could not turn him, but also knew,
We'd go again, we were not through.

Again made our round, brought out the stray,
And drove him straight through, the woods on that day.

And once again, you wouldn't believe,
He saw the gate, it made him leave.

Now by this time, we both were mad,
Our horses were hot, because we had,

Been out-run twice, it's time to show,
Him who's the boss, we are, you know!

My brother said, let's just stay cool,
And bring him out, and here's the rule,

When he turns back, to do his thing,
Take down your rope, and let it swing.

And if he goes, the other way,
I'll do the same, this is his day.

So it was time, to cowboy up,
Build a big loop, and try our luck.

And sure enough, just one more time,
We brought him out, he drove just fine.

And like a clock, just as before,
He made his dash, toward me, of course.

Shook out my loop, my horse in gear,
Wide-open fast, wind blew a tear.

That bull was close, I almost threw,
But then a crash, nothing to do,

But hit the ground, and wonder why,
My horse went down, while on the fly.

It turned out, that we didn't see,
A little wire fence, just meant for me.

Really well-hidden, by brush and weed,
Enough to trip us, when at that speed.

Of course that old bull, he got away,
And lived to play, another day.

And all that I got, was wounded pride,
By the bad ending, of that fast ride.

My brother thought, it was a big joke,
I was bruised bad, but nothing broke.

But the big lesson, I learned on that day,
When you are going, to get a wild stray.

You must be careful, or you'll get hurt,
And wind up sitting, bruised in the dirt.

Now I go preach, and serve the Lord.
And try to share, and teach His Word.

But there are folks, who won't turn and then,
Can cause you hurt, when you go for them.

We always should pray, and try to show,
The love that we have, so they will know.

But if you try, and they just don't care,
About the love, you're trying to share,

You're probably not, the one, don't you see,
To bring them back, so just let them be.

And pray God sends them, just the right one,
More able to show them, they should end their run.

"And whoever will not receive you nor hear your words, when you depart from that house or city, shake off the dust from your feet..." (Matt. 10:14)

Under God

I pray that our land, will someday be,
A place where we, once more can see,

The way God meant, for us to live,
And learn to be, the ones who give,

The praise that He, alone should get,
While those who served, we don't forget.

They fought and died, to make us free,
For justice, and for liberty.

They fought at first, in Lexington,
And Valley Forge, and old Bull Run.

At Gettysburg, and places where,
The nation had to heal its tear.

We rose to fight, the Kaiser too,
When that came up, knew what to do.

They fell at Pearl, and Pelaliu,
Iwo Jima, Okinawa, too.

And Hitler's reign, could not stand,
When Uncle Sam, raised his hand.

Korea then, and Viet Nam,
Kuwait and then, Afghanistan.

Fallujah never saw our back,
When we took the fight, to Iraq.

Through all of this, the people found,
When we Americans, come around,

We don't come, to fight and stay,
We do what's right, then go away.

And if there is, a storm or flood,
Earthquake, fire or shedding blood,

People know that we will come,
And do our best to help someone.

What we say and what we do,
Make a world where dreams come true.

Not so just a few can reign,
But so each can have the same,

Freedoms that God meant for all,
And have the chance for walking tall.

Some think it's not about our faith,
But more about the cash we make.

Or that it's just, we learned to fight,
Because we're strong, we think we're right.

For them the good old U.S.A.,
Is not so good, I've heard them say,

We built our prosperity,
On the backs of people, never free.

For them it's wrong we've done so well,
Because we gave the others hell.

But is that true? Can it be,
That we have such hypocrisy?

I say no, though sometimes wrong,
Our faith is what has made us strong.

We understand the thing that's true,
It's what our founding fathers knew,

That freedom is from God above,
And if we emphasize His love,

We will find that we can stay,
Strong and good in every way.

And for those who don't believe,
They have the right, to not receive,

The grace that makes our country strong,
And even though, we think they're wrong,

The beauty of a land this free,
No one will force them to agree.

But don't sit there and try to say,
We got here some other way.

Yes, we have our faults, it's true,
Weaknesses and troubles, too.

We fall and fail, and some will say,
The best is gone, we've lost our way.

But I still, believe we can,
Have revival in the land.

Turn to God, and praise His name,
Live so more can do the same.

For under God we'll always be,
Or lose our true identity.

Our faith is what made history,
But better still, our destiny!

"One nation under God, indivisible, with liberty and justice for all..."
(The Pledge of Allegiance)

Church

Cowboy: Should I go to church on Sunday, Lord?
God: Why do you ask?
Cowboy: Some people think it's really important. Is it?
God: Will it help you to be there? Will you help someone else?
Cowboy: Are You telling be to do it?
God: I think you know...

Runaway

Why all the pain, and suffering and tears?
Why are so many, cheated of years?

They could still be here, then tragedy struck,
And now they are gone, is it just about luck?

Don't have all the answers, and don't pretend to,
And I've had my share, of trouble it's true.

I have known people, whose children have died,
And cannot imagine, the tears that they cried.

I have seen sickness, raise its cruel hand,
Rob a man's strength, then take down the man.

I've been with those, who lost everything,
Left with their memories, and no song to sing.

Guess when you stop, to seriously think,
If you're not careful, you're apt to sink,

Into the deep valley, of fear and despair,
And wonder if even, the Lord above cares.

Yes, I have heard people, pray desperate prayers,
And ask if God hears, if He's really there.

I believe that He is, though I cannot say why,
Bad happens to people, and yes those who try,

To live the right way, and honor the Lord,
Obey His Spirit, and rely on His Word.

But even those people, can have heart-break,
And wonder if they, will be able to take,

The trials of life, that happen to them,
Without getting bitter, and discouraged within.

The pain that they feel's like a runaway horse,
Can't be reined in, too strong of course.

And all of the answers, that some people give,
Sound just like nonsense, to those trying to live,

Just through the day, forget the next two,
Holding on tight, don't know what to do.

Some say, God did it, and don't ask Him why,
Some tell you to wait, for pie in the sky.

Some that will tell you, that if things go wrong,
It's your lack of faith, that it is not strong.

Still others imply, that all of this stuff,
Happened because, you once lived so rough.

And now that it's coming, round to hurt you,
You ought to expect it, 'cause of what you used to.

One way or the other, you are at fault,
More faith, less sin, and now you're caught.

But is it really that simple, just cause and effect,
Or is some of this random, a worldly reflex.

Of course there's the devil, alive and well,
Spreading his poison, dragging to hell.

But he's not to blame, for all of these things,
Some of it's just with us, till heaven's bell rings.

They hurt you, then left, they cheated and lied,
They couldn't get well, and finally died.

They fired you, they used you, they were not real,
They pretended to be something, that they did not feel.

They stole your money, they wasted your time,
You fell for their story, you bought their line.

And then it all back-fired, and you lost your mind,
Can't see for the pain, and mad you were kind.

Or whatever else, has happened to you,
That destroys your peace, and steals every clue.

Maybe the answer, is we cannot know,
And just have to finally, let it all go,

Into the hands, of Someone who,
Knows all about us, and still loves us, too.

I've found when I really, surrender control,
Of the burden I carry, it relieves my soul.

And I can have peace, without knowing why,
Bad things still happen, and good people die.

We sometimes feel helpless, we want to try,
To fix all the problems, make every tear dry.

No, it is not easy, to let go of our stuff,
But if we don't do it, things really get tough.

And the misery will spread, to all those we know,
It doesn't just sit there, it gets worse and grows.

My favorite prayer, when I am in pain,
Is one that God hears, it's always the same.

And that's "Lord, have mercy," and sometimes for days,
That's all I can say, when I bow and pray.

But He's promised grace, to the humble, you see,
So don't miss the chance, to get some and be,

Lifted by Jesus, who understands you,
Relieve every burden, and all your care, too.

"Therefore humble yourselves under the mighty hand of God, that He may
exalt you in due time, casting all your care upon Him,
for He cares for you." (1 Peter 5:6-7)

Yonder

Yonder in the distance, just beyond what we can see,
Lies a pasture of God's making, He has sowed for you and me.

You can stand up in your stirrups, and take the longest view,
And if you're seeing clearly, you will know that it is true.

No, not all believe it, they are bound by earthly sight,
Insist we are mistaken, argue fiercely that they're right.

And no we cannot prove it, to those who think we're wrong,
Their doubt and cynicism, have been with them for so long.

But I have heard the music, and I have seen the light,
I have felt the power, and walked by faith, not sight.

The horses there are running, manes flying in the wind,
And they know that we're coming, when through with where we've been.

The cowboys have no tears there, they've all been wiped away,
By the Savior who is present, who brought them home to stay.

And even those who made it, though no one thought they would,
Received what Jesus offered, He let them know they could.

And some of those church people, who did not play it true,
Will wonder when He tells them, I never did know you.

But that never has to happen, to anyone, you see,
'Cause Jesus died to save us, set every captive free.

Give us living water, feed us living bread,
Grant us life eternal, that's what Jesus said.

The thing that every heart wants, the void we cannot fill,
Is something He will give us, His peace, that is the deal.

The river's running freely, it's all a dream come true,
It's running there forever, and waits for me and you.

I can see beyond the tragic, feel grace when there is pain,
And every time it happens, I'm reminded once again,

This life is not the reason, we exist at all,
We're going to the homeland, with all of those who call,

On Jesus as their Savior, and confess Him as their Lord,
Receive the Holy Spirit, build life upon His Word.

So, next time you see the sunset, with all the colors there,
Take a look beyond it, to the place that God will share.

Jesus said He was preparing, a place for us to be,
And when He gets it ready, He'll come and let us see.

And if our life is over, before He comes again,
If we've trusted Jesus, and know we've followed Him,

We can know the power, of heaven's open gate,
And have the full assurance, of our eternal fate.

"No eye has seen, no ear has heard, and no mind has imagined what God has prepared for those who love Him. But it was to us that God revealed these things by the Spirit..." (1 Cor. 2:9-10)

New Year

Cowboy: What should I do with the new year, Lord?
God: Just live it, son, one day at a time.
Cowboy: How?
God: Let me live through you.

When You Say Cowboy

When you say cowboy, what do you mean?
Are you talkin' 'bout someone, who's long, tall and lean?

Do you have a picture, of him in your mind?
Or is the question, a big waste of time?

For some it's all over, just yesterday's news,
And some think it's childish, to get down with the blues,

'Bout a culture that was, but will never more be,
And the people who lived it, are all dead, you see.

I hear what they're sayin,' and Lord knows it's true,
We got wanna-be cowboys, who don't know what to do.

Some bought a hat, and wear it with pride,
But don't ever ask them, to step on and ride.

Yes, some have the look, the swag and the charm,
But can't gather cattle, ain't worth a darn.

You really can't blame them, they just wanna be,
Though the real thing's elusive, not easy to see.

It's not just mystique, or a romantic view,
It's being effective, at what cowboys do.

'Cause when you say cowboy, it's a throwback to when,
There was no confusion, 'bout men who were men.

And when a man cowboyed, it was something he learned,
The work they assigned him, or else he got burned,

By the horse that was snorty, or the bull that ran wild,
The weather that fought him, and rarely was mild.

Yes, he learned from the ones, who were getting it done,
Else went back to town, some left on the run.

You see every real cowboy, has one quality,
That helped him to learn it, called humility.

Nobody who's cocky, or wants to be cool,
Will learn to be cowboy, they're too big a fool.

The cattle are out there, must be someone who,
Can make sure they're cared for, and husband them, too.

And when that old cowboy, finds someone who cares,
About learning the right way, he does want to share.

Whether he's a cowpuncher, from down Texas way,
Or from the Great Basin, where the buckaroos play.

All kinds of styles, that go with the work,
And no way to learn without blood, sweat and dirt.

Yes, some have the look, but can't learn the do,
Others look cowboy, and do it all, too.

Let's not forget cowgirls, out there working hard,
Learning to be top hand, and make a good pard.

We get down there with it, and just pay our dues,
Your ego gets stomped on, and in time you lose,

The need to impress folks, with all that you know,
No matter the progress, there's still far to go.

There's a big lesson, in all this you see,
'Bout what the Lord tells us, and wants us to be.

Not all can be cowboys, but we can all learn,
From mentors who've been there, and when it's our turn,

Pass on the good things, we know to be true,
Help those who will listen, to know what to do.

God's Word says He graces, those who will get low,
Humble themselves, and admit they don't know.

Resists all the proud ones, you can count on that, too.
The Book clearly says it, we know that it's true.

I guess what I'm saying, when you get past the bluff,
Of the ones who are posing, and pretend to be tough,

There's something deeper, to the real cowboy heart,
Something so strong, it will not fall apart.

It's about staying humble, thank the good Lord above,
For a life with God's creatures, and filled with His love.

Not all see this clearly, but more and more do,
And I am so thankful, that He saved me, too.

No, being a cowboy, won't get you saved,
Being born of the Spirit, only happens by faith.

And it's just my opinion, but I'll stand up and say,
That living for Jesus, is the real cowboy way.

"...God resists the proud, but gives grace to the humble..." (James 4:6)

Heaven

Cowboy: I'm so thankful, God, that Jesus died so that
we can get into heaven. This life can really be hard.

God: My Son didn't die just to get you into heaven.

Cowboy: What are You saying to me, God?

God: Jesus died not only to get you into heaven,
but to also get heaven into you.

Cowboy: Why is that so important?

God: Because the more heaven you get on the way to heaven,
the more people will want to go with you...

When I'm Wrong

It's hard to admit it, when I know I'm wrong,
I fear if I go there, I won't appear strong.

Sometimes it's uphill, to really come clean,
Tend to avoid it, if you know what I mean.

I know when I've blown it, the Spirit shows me,
And then I must choose, which way it will be.

Do I make excuses, or blame someone else,
Or really get honest, and admit to myself,

That I made a choice, that was up to me,
Disobeyed Jesus, acted selfishly.

We want "them" to think, we know what to do,
And if we don't do it, shows we are untrue.

And then they won't love us, or give us respect,
Because we can't achieve, all that they expect.

But is that what matters, is that what should be,
When problems won't leave us, and we cannot see,

The answers we need, for the pain that we feel,
And can't help but wonder, if anything's real.

I look at my horses, I watch as they feed,
They know they can trust me, to take care of their need.

I never would hurt them, and they know it, too,
And so they come to me, they're sure I'll be true.

I see there a lesson, when I have done wrong,
And allow my problems, to string me along.

I have a Master, who knows me and cares,
And clearly says to me, He'll always be there.

He died on that cross, so we can be free,
My sins all were nailed there, it's now up to me.

I should run to Jesus, where I find relief,
When I will confess, He gives me His peace.

And if I've hurt someone, and need to go see,
If they will accept, my apology,

He gives me the grace, to make all things right,
Rest in His answers, and walk in the light.

"If we confess our sins, He is faithful and just to forgive us our sins and to cleanse us from all unrighteousness." (1 John 1:9)

Stuff

Cowboy: Lord, Your Word is full of warning about owning stuff.
Problem is, I really like my stuff.
God: So, what's the question?
Cowboy: If I love you, do I have to give up my stuff?
God: No, but you have to give up something more important than that.
Cowboy: What is that, Lord?
God: You have to give up OWNING any of your stuff.
Cowboy: Why?
God: Because I really own it, and if you try to own it, it owns you.
Cowboy: Can I keep it, then, and maybe have more?
God: Only if you learn to be a steward, not an owner.
Then you're free to enjoy it, and even give it away.
Cowboy: What if I try to keep it and own it?
God: You stack the odds of losing it.
You only really have what you're willing to give...

Mountain Hide-out

When times get hard, as they sometimes do,
I saddle my horse, and I come to You.

I ride to a place, away from the noise,
From the clutter of life's work and toys.

My horse seems to know, when we're headed there.
Maybe he feels, what I need to share,

With the One who calls, from the throne of grace,
Jesus Christ, who took my place,

On a cruel cross, so long ago,
And now says come, let His grace flow.

I top the hill, and now I see,
That special place, where I want to be.

Unsaddle my pony, and hobble him right,
Throw down my roll, and start the fire-light.

Boil up some coffee, begin to think,
Of how we rise, and sometimes sink.

The wind blows through, the treetops there,
Cool, sweet water from a spring to share.

A hillside with a beautiful view,
Of the valley below, all green and blue.

I kick back and sip my cup,
As the stars come out, I look up.

And let my soul commune with Him,
Receive His peace, confess my sin.

By morning light I feel okay,
Saddle my pony and ride away.

I thank the Lord for a sweet retreat,
Where I can hear, the Lord's heartbeat.

And draw close, He lets me see,
How life with Him, is supposed to be.

No, I don't live, on a mountaintop.
My life is full, I cannot stop,

As often as I think I should,
But if I try, I maybe could,

Turn back to Him, deep in my heart,
And find the peace, for a brand-new start.

I love my mountain hiding-place,
On that high range, I've seen His face.

And heard the Lord, speak sweet and low,
And call me to His love, you know.

It's good to go, but better still,
To live each day, within His will.

And take the hope, He's given me,
To all who need to be set free.

"Be still and know that I am God." (Psalm 46:10)

Prayers

Cowboy: Lord, do You answer all prayers.
God: Why do you ask?
Cowboy: Because some of mine don't seem to be getting through.
God: I hear all of them. I just don't always give you the answer you expect or when you expect it.
Cowboy: Should I keep on praying?
God: Yes, son, you should.
Cowboy: Why?
God: Because I may not answer all prayers, but I do answer all pray-ers...

Thanksgiving

We give thanks to God our King, who blesses us with everything,
We need to know and do His will, and hear His voice when we are still.

I cannot count all He has done, to show Himself through His dear Son,
Yes, Jesus came and paid it all, to save us all from Adam's fall.

And heal each one so thoroughly, that we can know Him personally,
To be sure that we can see, and celebrate eternally.

I thank the Lord for this good land, and all who gave to make a stand,
For all the freedoms we hold dear, and what it took to never fear,

Those who would take them away, and stop the good old USA,
For patriots who gave their all, and answered yes when they were called.

I thank the Lord for family, and friends who mean so much to me.
For those who know me best of all, and still love me, never stall.

For sunsets with their golden glow, the satin moon that rises slow.
I praise Him for the scenery, that fills my heart and makes me see,

The broader sweep of heaven's brush, and never be in such a rush,
That I fail to thank the One, who's always there and gets it done.

I'm glad I've had Him there with me, when I was lost and could not see,
When I ran the devil's race, and could have died without a trace.

But I was spared, I know, it's true, 'cause He had plans for me to do,
Through lots of danger, trouble, too, but I survived and got a clue.

And He was there when my Dad died, to wipe away the tears I cried,
The prayers we prayed for children sick, and needed all His mercy quick.

Faithfully His love came through, He did what only He could do,
With grace sufficient in the trial, and then relief after awhile.

I thank Him for the horse I ride, the flowing mane and pacing stride.
And all the pleasure I have seen, the awesome places I have been.

There is so much more I could say, to write it down would take all day.
But I'll end this little rhyme, with praise that fills my heart each time,

I think of Him who died for me, His praises sing eternally,
And on this Thanksgiving Day, praise the Lord and to Him pray.

"In everything give thanks, for this the will of God in Christ Jesus
concerning you." (1 Thess. 5:18)

Scars
Cowboy: Lord, I have scars I don't want others to see.
God: Why?
Cowboy: I guess because they might not love me if they do.
God: My Son showed His scars after He was raised.
Cowboy: Why?
God: Scars give people hope. That's why showing them
             is worth the risk...

His Voice

The voice I hear, is what I need,
To do God's will, and pay no heed,

To what the world, tells me to do,
And always live, and tell the truth.

I have not known, that voice to raise,
It is not loud, with heavy base.

But much more like, a whisper low,
Telling me, which way to go.

It's something like, a cowboy who,
Speaks to his horse, on what to do.

And his mount, can learn his voice,
So he can make, the cowboy's choice.

He lifts the reins, and makes that sound,
That means let's go, and make a round.

The horse moves off, at just the pace,
The rider sets, and on his face,

There is a smile, because he knows,
His pony moves, and as he goes,

The two of them, they work as one,
To go and get the ranch work done.

I sometimes fail, to hear His voice,
I sometimes make, a foolish choice.

But one with Him, I want to be,
So that the job, gets done you see.

I want to be, more sensitive,
To the voice, that helps me live.

And gain the smile, I hope to see,
When I do, what He tells me.

"My sheep listen to My voice; I know them, and they follow Me." (John 10:27)

✻HB
G

Ride Away

I got on my horse, and just rode away,
Couldn't stand hearing, the words that they say.

The anger and drama, that some people need,
Don't care who they hurt, it's tragic indeed.

And having a way, to say things online,
Makes it no better, wastes everyone's time.

They're looking for fault, and this much is sure,
They always can find it, it's hard to endure.

The Bible says people, who let on this way,
Are headed for trouble, gets worse everyday.

They cannot be thankful, and just let things go,
Have to start something, and insist you know,

That it isn't their fault, they've turned out to be,
Such miserable people, who spread misery.

They need to know Jesus, and give Him their pain,
Lose sight of themselves, eternal life gain.

They could be happy, with His kind of peace.
If they surrender, they will find release.

You say they won't change, and maybe you're right,
But you never can tell, it could be tonight.

When God's grace hits someone, they find that it's true,
Christ died to heal them, and show what to do.

Some won't respond, they always say no,
But others repent, and then start to grow.

We pray for them all, and especially,
The hard ones to love, unconditionally.

So when I am tempted, to just ride away,
I think about Jesus, it helps me to stay.

"Dear friends, since God loved us that much,
we surely ought to love one another."
(1 John 4:11)

Thanksliving

Thanksgiving is over, we ate all the food,
Turkey and dressing, man, it was good!

We saw all the children, and grandchildren, too,
Laughed till we cried, trust me, it's true!

Watched all the ball games, our team didn't win,
But we're proud of them, next year try again.

Spent a few hours, horseback of course,
Makes me feel better, when I ride my horse.

Went to church Sunday, worshipped the Lord,
Prayed for each other, welcomed His Word.

And now it's all over, and we're on our way,
To a big Christmas, can't wait till that day.

But something inside me, will not let me go,
I'm sure I missed something, oh yes, I know.

Giving thanks to the Lord, is not just one day,
It's about praising, each step of the way.

From cradle to grave, and even past that,
Created to worship, now that's where it's at.

It is a great season, but when life is true,
It's done by thanksliving, each day God gives you.

"Let everything that has breath praise the Lord. Praise the Lord!"
(Ps. 150:5)

End of the Day

Sometimes I get, to the end of the day,
And wonder how it, so fast passed away.

I saw, then blinked, it was here, then gone,
Makes me feel, like something's wrong.

Sometime I think, my life's like that roll,
Of toilet paper, on this much I'm sold,

That the closer one gets, to the end of the line,
That thing rolls much faster, and so does our time!

I get out of bed, my joints creak and groan,
Yesterday's hurts, feel like some kind of loan,

That I must repay, with interest, you see,
And go on and do it, it's all up to me.

My time moves so quickly, I can't slow it down,
And sometimes it seems, I go round and round,

Doing the things, that I think I must do,
Without really asking, if I have been true,

To what really matters, and all of God's will,
'Cause I am running, and cannot be still.

There was a time when life's pace was slow,
Measured by seasons, not on the go.

It took more time, to get anywhere,
If wagon or horseback, was what got you there.

Folks lived close, to the land back then,
So long ago, Grand-daddy knew when.

If we could get back, to a much simpler life,
With less of the stress, and so much strife,

We'd probably find, we like it much more,
Be simpler to see, God's open door.

Back to the rhythms, of earth and sky,
Back to the horses, who always try,

To do just what, we ask of them,
Working alongside, with us as friends.

We've learned to make, our lives last long,
With science to keep us, fitter and strong.

But just adding days, to our lives won't do,
We must add more life to our days, too.

God says today, is what He will give,
We maximize it, by the way that we live.

We learn to love Him, with all that we've got,
And to love others, and by His grace not,

Waste one more day, He gives us to live,
On grudges and those, we refuse to forgive.

We can then learn, to do this life right,
Living each day, with His love in the light,

We'll know the joy, of having His smile,
And go to meet Him, in a short while.

A life that's worth living, we know that we can,
Focused on Jesus, and ride for His brand.

"For to me, living means living for Christ, and dying is even better."
(Phil. 1:21)

The Reins

Went to see Momma, not long ago,
She brought out her scrapbook, wanting to show,

Those many pictures, of me and my Dad,
To talk about memories, and times that we had.

Mom took a shot, of me at age three,
All decked out, a cowboy to be.

I sat on my pony, for the very first time,
There stood my father, still in his prime.

Her name was Sugar, a little old paint,
She was so gentle, I had no complaint.

Dad told me to frown, make my meanest face,
He made one, too, as he stood there in place.

Mom then described, that later that day,
Sugar got frightened, and then ran away.

I slid right off her, going full speed,
But Dad said get on her, 'cause he saw the need,

For getting back on, whenever you fall,
Don't let it stop you, you gotta ride tall.

And then as I sat there, thinking of that good plan,
I heard the Lord say, "Son, look at your hands."

I looked at the picture, much closer this time,
And there were my hands, I saw them just fine.

They held the reins, like Dad said to do,
But my heavenly Father, said something that's true.

"You've had the reins, in your hands a long time,
But if you'll let Me, I'll take them, they're Mine."

I remembered the worst times, that I ever had,
When I controlled things, they always went bad.

What a reminder, and I thank You, Lord,
Here are the reins to my life, I'll go toward,

All things You say, you want me to do,
I won't run away, or disobey You.

Said bye to Momma, had to go home,
But I will remember, when I'm tempted to roam,

That Jesus has promised, He will direct me,
If He has the reins, it's the best way to be.

"For all who are led by the Spirit of God are children of God."
(Romans 8:14)

Change Them

Cowboy: Will You please change them, Lord?
God: Why do you ask?
Cowboy: Because they really get on my nerves.
God: What if I used them to change you?
Cowboy: Are we talking about heavenly sandpaper again?
God: Only until I've smoothed off your rough edges...

A Friend

Everyone needs one, without a doubt,
Can't help thinking, it's what life is about.

All of life's pleasures, and all we go through,
Are much better shared, with one who loves you.

We all need a friend, who knows what to do,
Cry when we hurt, and laugh with us, too.

They're someone who knows us, can't spin it with them,
They listen intently, and know where we've been.

They would never judge us, still love when we're wrong,
But won't make excuses, when we should have been strong.

I've had some horses, I've counted as friends,
They helped me through heart-ache, this road's had some bends.

There were long nights alone, out under the stars,
When just my old pony, kept me out of the bars.

But a friend you can saddle, can just do so much,
We all need a brother, for that human touch.

Or a sister that cares, and will always be true,
She shows that she's loyal, and will stick right with you.

But even these people, who love us this way,
Have their own limits, with what they can say.

When it comes down to it, the One that we need,
Is the best friend forever, and so fit to lead.

'Cause He has been tempted, just like me and you,
Without ever sinning, did what His Father said do.

I'm speaking of Jesus, God's Son, of course,
Who sent us our best friends, and created the horse.

*☩BG

And when we know Him, as Savior and Lord,
He'll give us His friendship, it's there in His Word.

So if you are lonely, and need a good friend,
Turn to the Savior, His love has no end.

And you will know something, that few others do,
You're never alone, He's with you, it's true!

"...I have called you friends..." (John 15:15)

Surprise

Some things surprise me, I'll admit that it's true,
Thought I'd lived so long, I'd hear nothing that's new.

But again I am wrong, and I have to say,
I've seen some things, that shocked me today.

I heard the question, never thought they would say,
Should the national anthem, be heard when teams play?

Really? I thought, have we gone down so low,
We're ashamed of our flag, our love fail to show?

And what's all this talk, about what's right and wrong?
We call the bad good, and fail to be strong,

About having a compass, to show us the way,
And live with integrity, all of our days.

The heroes who served, we seem to forget,
And dismiss their suffering, as just a bad bet.

We claim we can tolerate, anyone's view,
But let someone say, that to Jesus they're true,

And they're ridiculed, for being a fool,
Just narrow-minded, and some right-wing tool.

I was not raised, in a city you see,
But out in the country, and working where we,

Still had belief, about what folks should do,
Learn to love God, and our country, too.

Though it's not perfect, I have to believe,
This country is blessed, and from God received,

The freedoms we cherish, the best way to be,
The God we believe in, gave us liberty.

Yes, I am surprised, by what I hear said,
But I hope change happens, before I am dead.

I want to see people, stand up for what's right,
Love one another, and walk in the light.

Is it all over? Is it too late?
For our America, to rise and be great?

I don't believe so, I know that it's true,
One nation under God, we still can do!

"You shall know the truth, and the truth shall set you free..." (John 8:32)

Complaint

Cowboy: Lord, I've had a lot go wrong lately. I feel like complaining.
God: I know how you feel. But you also have a lot to be thankful for.
Cowboy: So, Lord, should I complain or give thanks?
God: That's the choice you make everyday.

Horses

Of all God's creatures, great and small,
I like horses, I love 'em all.

I love the mustangs, wild and free,
Showing us all, what used to be.

The Clydesdales as they thunder by,
That beer commercial made me cry.

I love the hunter-jumpers too,
Precise dressage when it's true.

When polo ponies dart and wheel,
I'm really amazed by that deal.

I won't forget the smaller crew,
My little Shetland knew what to do.

And walking horses from Tennessee,
When we hunted, my Dad and me.

Endurance deep and desert-bred,
Arabians with their pretty head.

The thoroughbreds that run their race,
For the roses set the pace.

The bucking broncs in the rodeo,
Always put on quite a show.

Wagons pull and buggies, too,
Sleighs in winter just for you.

'Course I was raised, tending cows,
So quarter-horses taught me how,

To cut and rope and cowboy up,
Do the work and try my luck.

I never tire of watching them,
Drink or graze or work and then,

Saddle up and take my time,
On a day that works just fine.

And when I ride I give praise,
To God who uses this to raise,

My spirits when I'm feeling low,
And not sure which way to go.

And I know the day will come,
When Jesus takes His children home.

And when He does they say He'll ride,
A white horse from the other side.

It gives me comfort just to know,
That when it comes our time to go,

We'll be horseback with our Lord,
If we love and trust His Word.

"Blessed are the pure in heart, for they shall see God." (Matt. 5:8)

Saturday Night

Cowboy: It's Saturday night, Lord.
God: Yessir, it won't be long 'til Sunday.
Cowboy: Hope You'll help me behave tonight, Lord.
God: I will. What if I made you feel the same thing now that you feel after you misbehave?
Cowboy: That ought to do it. Thanks, Lord.
God: Anytime, son...

First Love

It was just like yesterday,
I met the Lord and heard Him say,

I suffered on that cross for you,
And that's when I really knew,

That I should just confess my sin,
Lose control and live for Him.

I had a strong break-through that day,
And He washed my sins away.

Filled me with His Spirit, too,
Began to show me what to do.

I learned from Him I couldn't stay,
With my old friends and games they play.

And I could not, go there again,
It would just, tempt me to sin.

I stayed with those, who helped me see,
All that God, had planned for me.

When I look back, to my first love,
I relied on power, from above.

He did through me, what I could not,
Trusted Him, to take a shot,

At sharing the good news I knew,
Pointing them to Jesus true.

I then went through a real hard time,
I fell away and lost my mind.

My hurts and pain caused me despair,
I drank so much I didn't care.

It took awhile for me to see,
That God had not done this to me.

I took His hand, and once again,
Got on the road and in the end,

I know I made a righteous choice,
To turn and hear my Savior's voice.

And now I preach and pastor, too,
Try to show folks what to do.

Many years have passed since then,
But I still remember when,

I found the Lord, then fell away,
Then found His love another day.

Just like a horse we trained and then,
His new owner abused him.

But when we got him back, you see,
He became the horse he used to be.

Never think that it's too late,
To find your Jesus-given fate.

If your heart beats, it's still true,
It is not too late for you.

Come and say where you have been,
Blame no one, confess your sin.

And you will find, that you will see,
All the love He gave to me.

"Nevertheless I have this against you, that you have left your first love..."
(Rev. 2:4)

Get It Done

The time does come, when you must do,
You cannot wait, it's always true,

That every shot, you do not take,
Will always miss, you cannot fake.

The Book of Life says don't just hear,
But do the Word, it's really clear.

Says those who only, watch the wind,
Never can, get their seed in.

And those who watch, for every storm,
Never reap, it is their norm.

If you want, to get ahead,
You cannot wait, 'cause lights are red.

They'll turn green, when you get there,
But only if, you go somewhere.

You cannot steer, a truck that's stalled,
No way to turn, but some are galled,

When they hear that, they must act,
Their mode is wait, and that's a fact.

They seem to think, the world owes them,
Entitled to, their every whim.

But that's just not, the way it is,
And surely those, who claim we're His,

Should go ahead, and take that shot,
We might miss, but then we've got,

Something from which, we can learn,
At least when comes, our next turn,

We know our aim, we might improve,
But not unless, we make our move.

I know the Good Book, says to wait,
Upon the Lord, but don't be late,

When it's time, to do His will,
Just go on, and don't be still.

It might just be, that God's the one,
Who waits for us to make our run.

We need to get out, of our box,
Do something that really rocks!

Dream big dreams, and then let go,
Pull the trigger, then we'll know,

That God will bless, a step of faith,
And course-correct, every mistake.

Everyone raised on the ranch,
Knows that you must take a chance,

And if we trust and do our part,
God sees every willing heart.

So don't just sit there on some shelf,
That horse will never train himself.

There's work to do, things need repair,
Waiting for someone who cares.

And there are people, all around,
Who need the love, that we have found.

And we are called to go, and then,
Not wait for them to be our friend.

Yes, we are called to get it done,
Love the Lord, and help someone.

"Farmers who wait for perfect weather never plant. If they watch every
cloud, they never harvest." (Ecclesiastes 11:4)

Words

The words we use, and how we talk,
Direct the course, of how we walk.

The Book of Life, says it is true,
That what we want, a horse to do,

Shows him when we use a bit,
Like a rudder on a ship.

Something small, like our tongue,
Determines how, the work gets done.

A tiny spark can light a fire,
Consequences great or dire.

And if we don't, show it control,
Viral goes, and on a roll,

To do things that, we never meant,
And go places never sent.

So much harm, that can be done,
So much good- either one,

Comes from such, a little source,
I'm speaking of the mouth of course.

Proverbs says the tongue can be,
The source of life or death you see.

So let's choose life by what we say,
And let's speak up and start today.

With all the things we wish we said,
Say it now before we're dead.

Speak the truth in love right now,
Trust the Lord, He'll show you how.

Always give encouragement,
To all those, to whom you're sent.

Get rid of all complaints and whines,
Learn to praise Him, all the time.

Don't get in the insult game,
Always bless in Jesus' name.

Remember what the Lord gave me,
When I failed to really see.

Said if the words you say all day,
Could be caught and held some way,

And then they poured the words on you,
When the day is finally through.

Would those words cleanse and heal,
Or make you hurt and dirty feel?

It was such a wake-up call,
I asked the Lord, forgive it all!

Speak Your words through me today,
Help me spread life, by what I say.

"We can make a large horse go wherever we want by means of a small bit
in his mouth..." (James 3:3)

Miracles

Cowboy: Why are there so few miracles, Lord?
God: What makes you think so?
Cowboy: I haven't seen many lately. Why?
God: Maybe you're looking for the wrong kind of miracle.
Cowboy: What kinds of miracles are there?
God: There are miracles that change everything.
            Everyone wants those.
Cowboy: What's the other kind?
God: The kind that don't change everything, they just change you.
            People don't like those as much...

A Baby

Stop and think, that when God came,
He chose this means, it was the same,

Way every one of us gets here,
We are born, so it is clear,

That God Himself would come that day,
So the prophets had to say.

A lowly virgin would give birth,
When One from heaven came to earth.

I've wondered would it be the same,
If in modern times He came.

Would the womb be just as safe,
When He came to take our place?

Thank God He came, that's all I know,
And I want to praise Him so.

'Cause He is called Emmanuel,
God with us, and He would tell,

The way of peace to all of us,
Save us from sins, this same Jesus.

Some do not believe it's so,
For them it's just an easy no,

To something they will not believe,
And so the truth they can't receive.

We're better off not to engage,
Those who idolize this age.

And want to start an argument,
About the One who's heaven-sent.

The Lord tells me, son, don't go there,
Just celebrate and show you care.

Leave the rest in Jesus' hands,
When they react to His demands.

The patience that the trainer shares,
When that colt, rebels and dares,

Him to do just one more thing,
He runs and bucks and has his fling.

But quietly the man persists,
Even when the horse resists.

And finally when all is done,
When the colt has had his run,

There is a moment they connect,
And from then on the deal is set.

And that's what God has done for all,
By coming as a baby small.

To patiently give all the light,
God in flesh, what a sight.

The baby that we sing about,
Came to cast the darkness out.

He grew up, and lived and died,
Rose again, for every tribe.

He left the glory, came to earth,
Was born to give us second birth.

"And the Word became flesh and dwelt among us..." (John 1:14)

Clean

Looks clean to me, that's what I said,
She disagreed, her look I read.

I looked again, I tried to think,
What could she mean, I sipped my drink.

She said she now could understand,
Why I was through, and on my can.

While she still worked at cleaning well,
It was right then, man, I could tell,

That I had missed a thing or two,
And there was lots more work to do.

Problem was, there was a game,
Don't quite remember that team's name,

But at the time I did not miss,
An important game like this.

Thought my case was strong, you see,
'Cause all the chores I'd done early.

Fed the horses, cattle, too,
Even swept the tack room through.

Washed some clothes and baby fed,
Changed the sheets on several beds.

Just had one more thing to tame,
Clean the bathroom, then the game.

Did the stuff I thought so well,
And if not, she couldn't tell.

But there I sat, and I was wrong,
That bathroom smell, was something strong.

The lesson learned in all of this,
Is one you can't afford to miss.

When you clean a toilet bowl,
Make sure you don't get on a roll,

And miss the parts that you should clean,
Else things can quickly get too mean.

The Lord might let you miss the game,
If your excuse, like mine, was lame.

"And whatever you do in word or deed, do all in the name of the Lord Jesus, giving thanks to God the Father through Him." (Col. 3:17)

Winners and Losers

Cowboy: Lord, do you make some people winners and some losers.
God: Why do you ask?
Cowboy: It just seems that way sometimes and I
         wondered if You somehow set it up that way?
God: I do not see people the way you do.
         I love them all the same,
         no matter how they are labeled on earth.
Cowboy: Okay, but wouldn't it look better for
         You if more people won?
God: What looks better isn't always actually better.
         In fact My Word says, "...whoever desires to save his life
         will lose it, but whoever loses his life for My sake will find it..."

Country Christmas

It tastes like cornbread, and pecan pie,
Ham and turkey, food piled high.

It smells like logs, in the fireplace,
Blazing up, to slow my pace.

It sounds like carols, old and new,
Jingle bells and choirs, too.

It feels like cold and blustery,
But inside hugs, and real cozy.

It's seeing smiles, on every face,
And going home, to find your place.

What we smell, and what we hear,
Reminds us Christmas is so near.

What we see, taste, feel comes back,
And helps us forget what we lack.

Give thanks to the Lord above,
For every blessing of His love.

We know they'll have, presents there,
Some we get, and those we share.

Santa comes and oh what joy,
When they open all those toys!

All the fun for every child,
Sometimes it gets loud and wild!

Gather 'round and read the Book,
Hear the story, take a look,

Once again at why we're here,
Hold the truth in our hearts dear.

Get up early, shoot the gun,
Man, we're gonna have some fun!

Later we'll get in a ride,
Saddle up and take our time.

Talk and laugh, and maybe sing,
Don't forget a single thing,

About how good, the Lord has been,
Sends His blessings even when,

We don't always, do what's right,
Follow Him, or spread the light.

And all of this, because He came,
As a baby, called His name,

Jesus, because He would save,
On the cross His life He gave.

And we want everyone to know,
Before it's time we have to go,

That we love them and we pray,
God will bless them everyday.

"..She wrapped Him snugly in strips of cloth, and laid Him in a manger..."
(Luke 2:7)

Rest

Say that again, what's that you say,
You won't believe it one more day?

Because the pain that you've been through,
Has stolen what you used to do.

It hurts so much and will not stop,
You walk the floor and watch the clock.

But time moves slow, the night is long,
And what has happened is so wrong,

You wonder if, the Lord is there,
And if He is, does He still care?

You catch your horse and saddle up,
Hoping to avoid the cup,

Of bitterness you drank so deep,
And loneliness that steals your sleep.

But even riding your best horse,
Makes you wonder if the course,

That your life has now become,
Should make you stay, or just run.

You make a round, clear your head,
Think about the words they said,

And wonder if you heard it right,
Or reacted with a fight.

Then while thinking what to do,
A verse comes calling just to you.

The words of Jesus to the weak,
Truth that only He can speak.

Telling you to come to Him,
Bringing all that does you in.

He will take the weight away,
Give hope for a better day.

His yoke easy, burden light,
So it's time, to end your flight.

Get the rest He offers you,
Realize His Word is true.

His love is patient, He will show,
Exactly the road you should go.

Heal you of the pain inside,
What you know you shouldn't hide.

All they did and how you feel,
Forgive it all so you can heal.

And choose to rest and trust in Him,
Let go of all that should have been.

"Come to Me, all you who are weary and carry heavy burdens, and I will
give you rest..." (Matt. 11:28)

Evil Men

Cowboy:	Lord, why do evil men prosper?
God:	Are you speaking of anyone in particular?
Cowboy:	No, I just wonder about it generally.
	Why do men who don't love you succeed?
God:	There are different reasons for different individuals.
	Sometimes my blessing leads them to salvation.
Cowboy:	What about the others?
God:	This is the only heaven they will ever see...

Let Go and Hold On

I let go the reins, they're in Your hands,
I hold onto Your will, I love Your commands.

I let go my hurt, I let go my pain,
I know You can heal me, I won't be the same.

I hold onto grace, I forgive every debt,
I won't let what they did, trip up my step.

I let go of habits, that once held me down,
I let go of thinking, I can't gain new ground.

I hold onto the Spirit, who gives me new life,
I count on His presence, to cast out my strife.

I let go of people, who steal all my dreams,
I let go their friendship, and all that it means.

I hold onto Jesus, who said He won't leave,
I claim every promise, and really believe.

I let go of the pride, that God must resist,
I let go my ego, and what it insists.

I hold onto knowing, that when I am weak,
Your power will be there, and reach its peak.

I let go the past, and what should have been,
I let go the future, and in the end,

I hold onto faith, that makes me sure,
That what I hold onto, will always endure.

"... I press on, that I may lay hold of that for which Christ Jesus laid hold of me..." (Phil. 3:12)

Moore

Moore is a good one, guess he'll always be,
This verse is for him, he's helped me to see,

When a cowboy gets older, and long in the tooth,
He has to get settled, with what is the truth.

His joints they are stiff, and all of those falls,
Leave him with arthritis, even if they were small.

'Cause you know you can't husband, the cattle, you see,
Without having wrecks, that can cause injury.

So now that he's older, he must ride that one,
That's old-man broke, but can still get it done.

He moves more deliberate, watches each step,
But if there's some trouble, you still need his help.

'Cause all that he's done, is still in his head,
And it isn't because, of the books that he's read.

He learned it the hard way, when the weather was cold,
Out doctoring cattle, stuff he's never told.

He roped a wild one, that no one could get,
On a day that was stormy, and muddy, and wet.

He caught those bulls, at that old water trap,
In country so dry, couldn't water a rat.

And topped off more broncs, that folks couldn't ride,
No way to count 'em, though some have tried.

He's stood up in his stirrups, on many hot days,
Searching the canyons, for lost and gone strays.

So if he moves slower, than all the young turks,
They should respect him, but if they are jerks,

They better not push him, an old man it's true,
Is too stiff to fight, he might draw and kill you.

No, I'm just foolin', the man loves the Lord.
He will forgive them, like it says in God's Word.

But all I am saying, and I know that it's true,
If you're feeling challenged, don't know what to do,

Call in the old cowboy, 'cause he's seen a lot,
And if you will ask him, he'll give all he's got.

"Counsel in the heart of man is like deep water, but a man of
understanding will draw it out." (Prov. 20:5)

Mercy

There is a promise, it's there in God's Word,
About daily mercy, it's straight from the Lord.

It says when each day comes, the sun shows its face,
Along with it rises, a day's worth of grace.

Yesterday had it, but now it's too late,
To do that day over, it's gone out the gate.

Tomorrow's not here yet, so we do not know,
What God will give us, till it's time to go.

We can get so bogged down, with our history,
Or worried and fearful, about our destiny,

We miss what God offers, on what's called "today,"
And then wonder why, we've lost our way.

It's like that old pony, who's so scared of you,
He forgets what the trainer, taught him to do.

He needs to remember, that all of his tasks,
Can be accomplished, and done well when asked.

He'll find that it's easy, to just get it done,
Much better to obey, than to buck and run.

No matter what happens, what God asks us to do,
He will empower, with His grace, it's true.

And when we are weakest, and feel most at risk,
Tempted to give up, and the devil insists,

That we are not worthy, or can't get it done,
He is a liar, and in the long run,

We won't fail Jesus, or lose our place,
If we lay hold of, God's daily grace.

"The faithful love of the Lord never ends! His mercies never cease.
Great is His faithfulness; His mercies begin afresh each morning."
(Lamentations 3:23)

The Horse I Need

I like to ride, with a slack rein,
A horse that won't is such a pain.

That lighter touch, and softer mouth,
Pleasures me with a smoother route.

I like a horse, that can be caught,
Won't run away, because he's taught.

I want my mount, to stand right there,
When I step on, I really care,

'Cause I don't like, to get on,
If he's moved, and almost gone.

I need a horse, that will back up,
He must reverse, just like my truck.

I want one that'll, stop and turn,
And doesn't balk, when he must learn,

The job that we want him to do,
To sort the cows, and rope them, too.

And when he goes, I want his head,
To not be flying, that's what I dread.

Like some horse, they jerked and pulled,
And ended up, as something culled.

Just downs his head, and pleasures on,
Relaxed and calmly, goes along.

He cannot always, look for ghosts,
Bolting when he thinks he's toast.

Not afraid of something new,
Because we've taught him what to do.

He needs to learn, to stand there tied,
And not pull back, and break the line.

And when it's time, to go somewhere,
Load on the trailer, without a care.

And be still, for the shoe-ing man,
That playfulness I cannot stand.

I like a horse, that will walk on,
Not go to sleep, but stays strong,

Works longer than, he wants to,
Because there is, so much to do.

Can't ride him down, can't steal his wind,
Because he's strong, and is your friend.

Friend, I said, I mean it, too,
With a horse, that's really true.

'Cause if you ride a counterfeit,
You deserve just what you get.

Whether spoiled, or never knew,
It's hard to teach him, what to do.

I've had some that did it all,
I gladly had them in my stall.

Trained them, and they made a horse,
Who made the cut, and stayed the course.

You know that horse who tracks a cow,
Reminds me of myself somehow.

The Lord has promised He will train,
No exceptions, all the same.

His disciples He will show,
How to change and how to grow.

He will teach us what to do,
Give us gifts, lead us in truth.

Fit us for the task ahead,
Supply our needs and keep us fed.

And just like the time we spend,
Getting horses right to send,

He will do just what we need,
Help us respond, so He can lead.

Lord, let us not be counterfeit,
But see Your will, and then do it.

"Loving God means keeping His commandments, and His commandments are not burdensome." (1 John 5:3)

My Friend

Cowboy: My friend was a Christian man, Lord.
Why did he have to die?

God: Death is a part of the human experience, son. Everyone dies.

Cowboy: Yes, but I guess I mean, why did he have to die so soon?

God: When my children end their earthly journey, death is a doorway to eternity. Even the longest lives on earth are a split-second compared to what happens after.

Cowboy: I miss him, Lord. Will You help me?

God: Yes, I will. And when you feel My presence with you, remember he's here with Me, where he always wanted to be...

Come Home

When it gets too hard, and you just don't know,
What you'll do, which way to go.

Your nerves are strained, your heart is broke,
Your mind feels like, you've had a stroke.

'Cause parts of you, aren't really there,
And sometimes you, don't even care.

Cannot sleep, don't eat too much,
Hard to work, just out of touch,

With all the things, you once enjoyed,
Because you feel, your life's destroyed.

You find no matter, what you drink,
You cannot change, the way you think.

And when you try to medicate,
It turns out, there's no escape.

The arms of someone, you don't know,
Can't heal the hurt, they only show,

How sad and empty, you've become,
And you won't turn, to just the One,

Who alone, can take away,
All the things that steal your day.

Just come to Him, it's not too late.
Your heart still beats, you should not wait.

Give all your pain to Jesus now,
And you'll find out, he helps somehow.

In ways that we can't always know,
To bring you some relief and so,

Don't stampede, and don't hold back,
The Lord will put your life on track.

And you'll be glad, that you found grace,
Received the smile, there on His face.

"Once you were like sheep who wandered away. But now you have turned
to your Shepherd, the Guardian of your souls." (1 Peter 2:25)

Return

Smell the soil, and grass that grew,
Cattle grazing, horses, too.

Out there where, the lights of town,
Can't be seen, nor the sound,

Of people running to and fro,
In a hurry as they go.

I grew up there, I'll go back,
When dues are paid, and all I lack,

Is knowing that, God says okay,
And when He does, He'll make a way.

The reason why, I think it's so,
Is in spite of where I go,

I always think of there as home,
And when I'm through, I will come,

To the simple life again,
Take off my watch and cell phone then.

Take a breath of country air,
And drop my heavy load of care.

Saddle up and take my time,
Trot on out across the line,

Of what I think and know and feel,
Reacquaint with something real.

That has no link, to a routine,
Except for nature's changing scene.

And find the joy of sun and rain,
Moon and stars, escape the strain,

Of all the drama and the scheme,
Of hurting folks to get your dream.

It's not that I don't love my life,
Or that my days are filled with strife.

It's just that I am still surprised,
That my life has been comprised,

Of all the time I've spent in town,
With so many folks around.

The Lord has sent me to reach them,
But someday that job will end.

And when it does, I will not cry,
But with peace, say my good-bye.

And go to that much slower pace,
In a more secluded place.

"So there is a special rest still waiting for the people of God..." (Heb. 4:9)

Art by Bruce Brannen

Speck

I caught a glimpse, of him as he flew,
Down off the ridge, and then I knew,

He was just gonna be, one of those steers,
That we had tried for, and missed many years.

My guess is seven, or eight years old,
Could be the one, that last year they sold.

But he broke the ropes, with which he was tied,
And slipped away, to the canyons to hide.

Because of the spots, that covered his hide,
They named his Speck, no one really tried,

To go and catch him, just too much to do,
With all the livestock, and horses, it's true.

No one had seen him, in a whole year,
Some even wondered, if he was still here.

Thought maybe the wolves, or a cat brought him down,
Then there he was, and without a sound,

Gone and then off, to some brushy hide-out,
Unless we find him, without a doubt,

We might not ever, see him again,
Just so well-hid, who knows where he's been?

I thought that I'd go, and take a look-see,
The cow boss okayed it, and mentioned that he,

Thought maybe the best way, was lay my bed-roll,
Near that old spring, that was his water hole.

'Cause all of God's creatures, both great and small,
Have to drink water, if they live at all.

Got off the grid, and made me a fire,
Warmed up some beans, before I retired.

Made a day's ride, when it got light,
Rode into the canyon, got set for the night.

Hobbled old Dan, with the spring nearby,
Thought I'd watch close, and give it a try,

Kept my rope handy, to throw if he came,
Dally off to a post oak, if true was my aim.

And sure enough after, the moon had its rise,
There were some cattle, and to my surprise,

A giant steer with 'em, all spotted with red,
One broken horn, on the side of his head.

Yes, he was the one, we were trying to get,
And so I waited, for him to get wet.

Then, just as gently, and quiet as I could,
I lifted my lasso, and moved where he stood,

In knee-deep water, he drank so deep,
He did not smell me, or hear my creep.

In a split second, I let my loop fly,
Over his horn and neck it did lie,

And just as fast, I took a quick wrap,
Round a stout post oak, and that was that!

I whooped and hollered, old Speck was caught,
I was the one, who'd caught him, I thought.

But then as I watched, I was amazed,
Speck kicked up his heels, lay down in a daze.

The rope it was cutting off, all of his wind,
He was a goner, unless I loosed him.

I cut my rope, a new one, it's true,
Old Speck just stood there, didn't know what to do.

Then off he trotted, and I shook my head,
Just got in my bedroll, and went on to bed.

Guess he's still out there, I don't really know.
But if you ask me, it's better to show,

Mercy to one, who's there in a bind,
Than be the one, who wins every time.

And it's not just critters, I'm talking about,
But people who get caught, and have no way out.

Maybe we give them, just one more chance,
To find forgiveness, and join the dance.

I'd rather be known, for the mercy I give,
The grace that I offer, by the way that I live.

"Blessed are the merciful, for they shall obtain mercy..." (Matt. 5:7)

Disagree

Cowboy: What do I say, Lord, to people who say I don't love them if I disagree with them?
God: Ask them if they love their children.
Cowboy: Why?
God: Because almost everyone loves their own kids.
Cowboy: And when they say "Yes, I love my children," what do I say?
God: Ask them if their children ever do things they disagree with.
Cowboy: I see what You mean.
God: Love in its highest form is unconditional. But love never means a blanket approval of whatever someone does. I love everyone, but I often disagree with their choices...

Boundaries

What do you think about that, he said,
In a tone of voice I'd come to dread.

The question was not true, you see,
'Cause with my words he disagreed.

No matter what- both yes or no,
The other side was what he chose.

And so I learned to silent be,
Let him talk and vent so free.

Have you worked, with one like that,
Who argue when you drop your hat?

Contentious, loud, and in control,
Don't ever stop, they're on a roll.

I say get away from them,
Quickly walk or run or swim,

Whatever route, you must take,
Get a plan and then escape.

It's like when you, buck off that bull,
You don't just hope that he is dull.

You move so fast to get away,
None on earth could make you stay.

And if that crazy heifer's wild,
You don't act like some sweet child.

You sort her out and make her go,
'Cause truth is she will likely grow,

A calf that acts like her, just worse,
And you cannot escape the curse.

And if that bronc, cannot be trained,
And you've nearly bruised and maimed,

Everyone that got on him,
It might be time to sink or swim.

Sell him to a rough stock string,
Replace him with a different dream.

A horse that has the sense to know,
That he'll enjoy the way you go.

And not fight you all the way,
Wants to learn and make your day.

We have to find God's boundary,
Though sometimes it is hard to see.

But if we don't, we go too far,
Hoping they can heal their scar.

And if you've ever worked with one,
Who only wants to hurt someone.

You will learn that it is true,
There's just so much that you can do.

"...Come out from among them and be separate, says the Lord..."
(2 Cor. 2:17)

Buckaroo

Jeans turned up, just a cuff,
Punchy chinks, all stained and rough.

Wild rag knotted at the neck,
Faded silk, what you'd expect.

Flannel shirt with double snaps,
Buckskin gloves to take his wraps.

Wrangler jacket, fish slicker, too,
Ready for the work to do.

And on top of his bald head,
Flat-brimmed hat, was all he said.

The boots were tall and buckaroo,
Jingle bobs on his spurs, too.

So what you get a picture of,
Is someone whom you gotta love.

Because you know that it is true,
Some have the look, but cannot do.

But something you can count upon,
That if you look at, the long run,

While others may, get down and do,
They have no style, to which they're true.

I am glad, there're still a few,
Who have the look, and do the do.

Just one more thing, that's left to say,
About all those who choose the way,

Christ intends for us to live,
And understand all we should give,

Have the look of the real thing,
Then match it when it's time to bring,

What you show, and how you act,
Should point to Him, now that's a fact!

"Thus also faith by itself, if it does not have works, is dead." (James 2:17)

Today

Just a young cowboy, but he caught my eye,
Something about him, brought up a sigh.

'Cause the way he rode past, all bold and free,
Made me remember, how I used to be.

His horse was a buckskin, His rig buckaroo,
His spurs were a-jingling, he knew what to do.

Round his neck was a wild rag, with cuffs on his wrists,
Coiled up reata, romal reins in his fists.

He glanced over at me, as he loped by,
Tipped his sombrero, and not a bit shy.

I thought of the days, when my only plan,
Was rope my horse early, and ride with the band.

It's not really over, but yesterday's dreams,
Flew by so quickly, stampeded it seems.

You can't get them back, that's what they say,
But maybe it's better, to just live today.

Yesterday's gone, we'd best let it go,
Tomorrow's not promised, and until it shows,

Remember today, is a gift from above,
And what we do with it, shows Him our love.

Be thankful and prayerful, forgiving and true,
And don't waste a minute, of what He gives you.

Stop all this wishing, about yesterday,
And give Him tomorrow, it's really okay.

This morning you woke up, this day He gave you,
Live life on purpose, it's what we should do.

"So teach us to number our days, that we may
gain a heart of wisdom." (Ps. 90:12)

Ego

Don't always know how, to do what's right,
To honestly, humbly walk in the light.

There's so much self, in me it seems,
My ego even, invades my dreams.

Paul said it best, when he admits,
His mind would often, give him such fits.

Inside he wanted, to get things right,
But on the down side, he'd have a fight.

And I admit I feel, just the same way,
I love the Lord, but still want to stray.

It seems that exactly, at the same time,
Old self wants to buck, fight the Spirit's line.

Sometimes I really, get right and then,
Know by God's grace, that I can win.

But then I can turn, around and just fall,
Into the sin, and my progress stall.

I'm like that horse, that's been well-trained,
Knows how to mind, but plays the game,

Of being snorty, now and again,
Just to check out, if he still can.

When I see the cross, of Jesus I sink,
Onto my knees, and always think,

Why on God's earth, am I this way,
Then I hear words, from the Spirit say,

Learn to lean on Me, and try to stay,
Focused on My pow'r, make it all day.

And I promise I will, always live through,
And do the things, that you cannot do.

Die to the old self, and trust in Me,
That's when a miracle, you will soon see.

"I have been crucified with Christ; it is no longer I who live, but Christ
who lives in me..." (Gal. 2:20)

We Know

When it really happens, you know that it's true,
That what the Word promised, has happened to you.

It's based on the knowledge, that you have His love,
And you can believe in, the grace from above.

I've seen those who show it, when training a colt.
Instead of abusing, and giving a jolt,

They just work him quietly, and gently they prod,
It's just like the Spirit, who turns us to God.

With gentle persistence, He calmly works on,
Giving us time, to accept what He's done.

And just like the colt, who finally learns,
We're not gonna hurt him, or make him feel burned.

God lets us know, that we will be fine,
If we trust in His training, He'll always be kind.

That love gets inside us, forgives and heals, too,
Puts all in perspective, tells us what to do.

We know there is nothing, that we can do right,
To increase His love for us, there's grace in His sight.

And all of our sinning, and things we've done wrong,
Can't take His love from us, because it's so strong.

The life-changing love, that I'm talking about,
Gives us assurance, and casts the fear out.

When you know that you have it, it will not let go,
You want it to change you, you pray it will grow.

Don't keep it a secret, not too good to be true,
He'll do for others, all He's done for you!

"We know how much God loves us, and we have put our trust in His love."
(1 John 4:16)

God's Yes

When I was a child, and thought of the Lord,
I thought He was angry, and His only word,

To me and the places, I wanted to go,
Would ever and always, be a firm "No."

Why did I think it? Not really sure,
But when you believe it, it's hard to endure.

'Cause you don't get it, that God above all,
Is love and kindness, and when we fall,

He's not out to hurt, or condemn what we do,
He just wants to save, and love us, it's true.

Like with that old pony, who disappoints you,
Though he's real pretty, but will not be true.

It's 'cause someone hurt, and abused him, you see,
Then culled him, and sold him, now he's turned out to be,

A horse who won't give, what you want him to show,
'Cause all he has ever, known is a "No."

There is a great verse, it's there in the Book,
It talks about Jesus, you should take a look.

It says that the Savior, will give us His best,
If we only see, that He is God's "Yes."

Yes, I forgive you. Yes, I heal, too.
Yes, I will show you, what you should do.

And though there are "No's," you should also obey,
If you follow my "Yes," you will sure be okay.

So hear the "Yes," because when it's clear,
You will honor His "No," 'cause the "Yes" is so dear.

It's a great thing to know it, you can count on it, too.
That God's love is saying, "Yes" just to you.

"...For all of God's promises have been fulfilled in Christ with a
resounding 'Yes!'"... (2 Cor. 1:20)

Jesus True

There is a song, they like to sing,
About the Lord, the King of kings.

That says He is, cowboy at heart,
But I'm not sure, about that part.

Yes, I proclaim, He made all this,
Open spaces, are all His.

And when there is, a long sunset,
He made the colors, don't forget.

And every horse, I ever knew,
In some way taught me, to be true,

To One who loves, and died for me,
And rose again, so we could see,

That life is what, He wants to give,
Cleanse our sins, and let us live,

In fellowship, with Him each day,
And follow Him, in every way.

It's not that I don't, understand,
What others mean, what really can,

Be a way, to share the truth,
And help us know, just what to do.

He was born, in a little barn,
It's written down, it's not a yarn.

And when it says, He'll come again,
A white horse, He'll ride and then,

Make sure His kids, are gathered in,
With Him eternity to spend.

But just a cowboy, I don't know,
Let us just make sure to show,

The truth of who, He really is,
So people can remember this,

And clearly see, the Savior's love,
And all He offers, from above.

"May you experience the love of Christ, though it is too great to
understand fully..." (Eph. 3:19)

Will I Be a Cowboy?

Will I be a cowboy, after I die,
Or will I be changed, in the sweet bye and bye?

Not really sure, no one can say,
But when Christ comes, He'll be horseback that day.

He'll ride a big white one, we don't know his name,
But that's how He's coming, all just the same.

And all those with Him, they're mounted up, too,
Riding white horses, I've read it, it's true.

With that many horses, it just seems to me,
They could use some wranglers, and just possibly,

That heaven's remuda, might need some care,
At the last round-up, so many are there.

Not saying they're snorty, or cold-backed or humpy,
With all that commotion, won't even get jumpy.

Won't need to lunge 'em, or sack 'em out,
No need to pony, or lope 'em about.

My guess is those horses, will know what to do,
'Cause Jesus won't have 'em, unless they are true.

But with that many, thousands they say,
Lined up for Grand Entry, on Jesus' big day,

The Lord might just say, now ya'll keep an eye,
On all these horses, up here in the sky.

I 'spect we'll look up, and what will we see,
Roy Rogers, Dale Evans, and there's Gene Autry.

There's Freckles and Lane, and oh, looka there,
A whole lot more cowboys, they're from everywhere.

John Wayne, Ben Johnson, and old Chris LeDoux,
And so many others, we just named a few.

They'll stand up in their stirrups, all praising the Lord,
Thunder down with Him, just like in God's Word.

When's all said and done, the thing that means most,
Is that we're saved, and in Jesus' boast.

Put our trust in Jesus, be washed in the blood,
Just get it settled, we really should.

Heaven's range will be bigger, than any we've seen,
The weather is perfect, the water is clean.

Whatever He's planned, for heaven to be,
It will be more, than all we now see.

But if God allows it, I sure hope it's true,
That I can still cowboy, beyond the blue.

"...No eye has seen, no ear has heard, and no mind has imagined what God
has prepared for those who love Him..." (1 Cor. 2:9)

Horseback Gospel Testimonies

1. Larry Mahan - Sunset, TX - "Brad, thank you for the messages. Your HBG is an impressive and well-done site. I'm sure it will be a success."

2. Nancy Lemons - Cookville, TN - "I haven't been subscribed to this page very long but I'm loving it. It's nice to see good 'ol country folks speaking the gospel in plain English. Thanks, Brad."

3. Ben - Lodi, NY - "I give my life to You, Lord, and ride for Your brand on the long haul."

4. Donna - Michigan - "I love this page. God bless!"

5. Ronnie Clark - Colorado City, TX - "Please continue in God's will. I believe He is using this ministry to reach people that might not be reachable by any other means. You have been a great blessing to me."

6. Robin Carrier - Ft. Collins, CO - "Brad, awesome ministry. When Steve needs alone time with the Lord he and his horse, Dixie, head west of our ranch to the mountains. He comes home stress-free and ready to go."

7. Jamie Lucario - Edmond, OK - "I recently turned my life over to God and this is JUST what I needed."

8. Anna Would - Vancouver, BC - "I just recently found your page through a friend and I am so encouraged by it! So glad to be a part of this page. I will be praying and also telling my friends about this site!

9. Marlo Mello - Big Island, HI - "Amen...God is a great God! Aloooooha from the Big Island, Hawaii! Blessings sent your way...thank you for all you do."

10. Aledo Chesmore - Henderson, NV - "I am putting you up there with Charles Stanley! Now I read you both and start my day with a smile. The Lord has blessed me indeed. My three horses say hi as well."

11. Cowboy Church Fans - 'Thanks, Brad. Found your page through someone who "likes" ours. Pray God will reach more for Jesus and that those who are His will learn to love and obey Him and be used by Him."

12. Bernie Neu - NY - "Enjoy your posts, so much good counsel and great pictures. Long live 'Horseback Gospel' and the Christian cowboys who inspire it."

13. Deric Cline - Elberta, AL - "I share all your posts. Thank you for sharing the gospel of Jesus Christ."

14. Bobby Ray Burnett - Cherokee, TX - "Thank you for your spiritual guidance and support!"

15. Fern Leavens-Kernelson - Sundre, Alberta - "I love this page and share it with my FB friends."

16. Nickie Perez - Sacramento, CA - "Praise the Lord. Thanks for sharing. I enjoy all your posts.

17. Judy Hackett Hall - Chico, CA - "HBG reaches out to people who need Jesus plus inspires and teaches all us believers."

18. Gene Haire - Waldo, Arkansas - "I look forward to reading your posts everyday and love reading God's Word. It's the best way to start the day."

19. Maurie Farr - San Angelo, TX - "I love that you share these scriptures, and the artworks are incredible."

20. Jon Hickox - Osino, NV - "Thank you for your great and uplifting poetry. May God bless you."

21. Johnny Sperry - Salt Lake City, UT - "I like these God-fearing, Bible-believing, Jesus-loving cowboys."

22. Fay Stinson - Greenville, AL - "Some days I read these and it's as if it were meant just for me. Thanks for sharing."

23. Greg Heideman - Seattle, WA - "...This is a must read..."

24. Huey Hoss Mack - Robertsdale, AL - "One of your best, my brother. My heart, His grace; His glory, my soon eternal story."

25. Jean Sissell - Nixa, MO - "Awesome! Love the scripture and the picture!"

Photo by: Jeff Tesney

Brad McClain Bio

Brad McClain's degrees include a B.A. from Texas Wesleyan University in Fort Worth, Texas and a Master of Divinity from Candler School of Theology at Emory University in Atlanta, Georgia. He has over thirty years experience in Christian ministry, and is currently pastor of Graceport Church, a nondenominational congregation on the gulf coast of Alabama.

Brad's background in the cattle business and passion for horses has found an expanding ministry expression through *Horseback Gospel*. The McClains have six children and eight grandchildren, and make their home in Montrose, Alabama on the beautiful eastern shore of Mobile Bay.

Contact Brad by emailing: revbradmcclain@aol.com.

Mailing Address:
P.O. Box 609
Montrose, Alabama 36559

www.BradMcClainMinistries.com

email: revbradmcclain@aol.com

www.HorsebackGospel.com

www.facebook.com/horsebackgospel

251-423-3882

CPSIA information can be obtained at www.ICGtesting.com
Printed in the USA
LVOW07s0003151015

458296LV00007B/26/P